Introduction
to
Computer Science

version 2.0

Robert Strandh

September 2012

Contents

Chapter 1

Introduction

1.1 Audicence

This book is meant for students who have contemplated higher studies in computer science but who have not yet made a final decision, but also for students who have dismissed computer science as their subject of study, but perhaps for the wrong reason, and of course for students who are still open to a wide range of candidate subjects for higher studies. The purpose of the book is to give a good idea of what kind of problems people working in various disciplines related to computer science, information technology, programming, and software engineering are asked to solve. Therefore, the book is particularly meant for those who know very little about what it means to study any of those disciplines, and in particular for those who might have a distorted idea of what the practitioners of those disciplines do.

1.2 What is computer science?

It turns out that it is somewhat difficult to understand what computer science *is* and what the people practicing this discipline *do*. First, let us try to find out what computer science is *not*.

Let us start with a famous quotation:

> Computer science is no more about computers than astronomy is
> about telescopes. – M. R. Fellows and I. Parberry[1]

From this quotation, we learn that computer science has nothing to do with computers. This might seem a bit odd, given that the word "computer" is part of the name of the discipline.

Next, let us examine a quotation from an online dictionary that defines the word "science":

> Knowledge or a system of knowledge covering general truths or the
> operation of general laws especially as obtained and tested through
> the scientific method and concerned with the physical world and its
> phenomena. – Merriam-Webster online dictionary.

And just to be thorough, let us also include the definition of "scientific method" from the same place:

> Principles and procedures for the systematic pursuit of knowledge
> involving the recognition and formulation of a problem, the collec-
> tion of data through observation and experiment, and the formu-
> lation and testing of hypotheses. – Merriam-Webster online dictio-
> nary.

The last two quotations tell us that computer science is not a science either, because it does not use the scientific method to formulate and test hypotheses about the real world.

So if computer science is not about computers and is not a science, then what is it, and why was it named that way? Let us start with the second question. We believe that there is a tendency to use the word "science" to mean something

---

[1]This quotation has often been attributed to a famous computer scientist named Edsger Dijkstra, but that attribution is in fact wrong.

roughly equivalent to "good stuff". People who use it that way get offended when they are told "computer science is not a science", because to them, that sounds like "computer science is not good". We obviously disagree.

In fact, there is another discipline that is not a science according to the quotations above, and that is *mathematics*. Like computer science, mathematics does not formulate and test hypotheses about the real world. Instead, it is one of the few disciplines that has the luxury of *creating its own worlds* and then studying those worlds. It so happens that some of the worlds created by mathematicians are close enough to the real world that the results of mathematics are highly applicable to the real world.

Computer science, like mathematics, is another discipline that has the luxury of creating its own worlds and then studying those worlds. Luckily, those worlds are sometimes sufficiently close to the real world, that the methods of computer science are applicable to the real world, in this case to the way computers, and in particular the software that runs on those computers behave.

But things get more complicated, concerning what computer science really is. In the 1970s, the need for university-educated programmers and software engineers started growing, and at the time, the only existing departments that were capable of taking on this demand were the departments of computer science. They gladly accepted this new responsibility, because it meant a steady growth of enrollments with new funds to go with them. But these new responsibilities also transformed the areas of interest of those departments, simply because the demand was for people with knowledge about pragmatic aspects of software and computers such as:

- programming and particular programming languages,
- computer architecture,
- operating systems,
- data bases,
- software engineering.

These areas were not part of the initial domains of computer science, and in fact, teachers and researchers in computer science departments frequently had little or no knowledge about these areas, but that is a subject that is of little interest to us here.

So, while initially, computer science was a discipline that studies the foundations and theory of software, it has lately come to mean a discipline that studies a variety of areas related to computers and to the software that runs on those computers. These areas include, but are not limited to:

- Theory, including computability and complexity theory, graph theory, some aspects of combinatorics, logic, formal semantics, etc.

- Programming *paradigms*, such as *imperative, functional, object-oriented, declarative*, etc.

- Programming languages, both specific existing languages and the creation of new languages.

- Software architecture, i.e., how to organize a large program into modules so as to make it easier to understand and maintain.

- Software engineering, which covers social, organizational, management, and economic aspects of software development as well as technical methods for developing large software systems.

- Algorithms and data structures, which deals with how to organize data in the memory of a computer, and how to obtain efficient methods for accessing and modifying such data.

- Data bases, an area that covers performance and safety issues of large data volumes on secondary storage devices, together with the methods and languages for accessing such data.

- Operating systems, which covers techniques and algorithms for creating and analyzing operating systems.

- Compiler techniques, which includes techniques and algorithms for translating high-level programming languages into machine code.

- Computer graphics, that covers methods for analysis, processing, and synthesis of images.

- Sound processing, with methods for analysis, processing, and synthesis of sound.

- Some aspects of digital signal processing, and control theory.

- Some aspects of interface design, interaction design, usability, and ergonomics as related to software.

- Formal specification and formal verification methods for software.

- Networking and distributed computing.

- Artificial intelligence, which covers search methods, knowledge representation, computer vision, etc.

- Computational geometry with algorithms and data structures for processing geometric forms.

- Computational linguistics, including language understanding and translation.

- Digital encryption and digital signatures.

Many countries where English is not an official language use a more accurate name for this discipline. For instance, in French, the departments that practice the areas listed above are called "informatique", and some English speakers have started using "informatics" for this discipline.

Computer science is a very exciting discipline, because for the past decades, it has had a tendency to take on the objectives of other disciplines, to apply and develop methods that are well adapted to the new problems but that use techniques that are "natural" to computer scientists, and by doing so, to make enormous progress in those disciplines. For example:

- Archeology. Traditionally, archaeologists document a site by drawing diagrams of the positions of all the different objects that are found. Now, they can take digital pictures, using a camera or a cellphone, from any angle and any distance. Digital methods then process those images to construct a three-dimensional model of the site and even analyze the objects in those pictures.

- Medicine. Techniques such as MRI and CAT crucially depend on methods from computer science to keep radiation doses down, while improving the accuracy of the results, and presenting images to medically trained staff.

- Architecture. three-dimensional modeling is an inexpensive method that allows architects to visualize the final design at low cost, and even to make virtual walks inside and outside edifices that do not yet exist.

- Acoustics. Designs of concert halls and operas can now be tested with respect to their acoustics long before construction begins.

- Engineering. Thanks to digital models, various artifacts such as automobiles can be designed faster and at a lower cost, while at the same time the safety of the final product is increased.

- Graphic art.

- Music.

The list could be extended with pretty much every active area of science, technology, engineering, sociology, history, arts, etc.

1.3   Why study computer science?

In this section, we give some good reasons for studying computer science. In fact, we give good reasons both for choosing a career in one of the areas of computer science, and for studying computer science as a practitioner of some other discipline such as physics, chemistry, mathematics, biology, geology, electrical engineering, mechanical engineering, etc.

First of all, we give some good reasons to choose a career in one of the areas of computer science. One such good reason is that it gives guaranteed job opportunities. The software industry increases every year and shows no signs of slowing down. The economy of most western countries is no longer driven by manufacturing of physical objects, but by creation of software. The reason for this is of course that more and more devices are controlled by software, and the software gets more and more sophisticated every year. Also, traditional manufacturing industries such as the automobile industry or the home-appliance industry hire more and more software staff. The reason is of course that their products contain an ever-increasing part consisting of digital electronics, and that part is controlled by software. In order to create this software, the traditional industries need more and more staff trained in domains such as programming, software engineering, compiler technology, algorithms, etc. As these products become more complex, only people with good knowledge in these domains will be able to produce the software required in the manufactured products, and so people trained in computer science will be crucial for producing the end products as well.

Many potential students of computer science are turned off by the image of the practitioners as spending 50-60 hours per week working with a keyboard and a computer monitor, without ever seeing the light of day, and without any contacts with colleagues, friends, or family. On the contrary, people working in the software domain spend most of their time in contact with other people, such as customers, end users, suppliers, managers, and of course with their team colleagues. Frequently, these contacts take place internationally, which gives the opportunity for travel. There is room for people who *prefer* to spend time with a keyboard and a monitor, but that is not the typical situation.

Now, let us try to answer the question as to why someone with a career in some domain other than computer science might want to study computer science. As it turns out, more and more domains use computer-based *tools*, from simple office software such as word processors to advanced tools for computer-aided design. Even domains such as music, graphic art, typesetting, etc., require the use of more and more sophisticated software. While it is possible to use these tools naively, doing so frequently makes the work very repetitive. The more sophisticated features of these tools often have a component that resembles programming, i.e., they allow the user to *automate* many of the repetitive tasks. To use such tools efficiently, the user can benefit from training in programming. In particular, when users become skilled, they might create little personal libraries of so-called *macros* that simplify their tasks. They might even start writing macros that are so generally useful that they can be *shared* among colleagues. This is a typical situation, and users without formal training in computer science will soon find themselves swamped with demands for fixes and added functionality. Managing such demands requires training in computer science. Furthermore, it can be argued that users *must* take advantage of the ability of these tools to be programmed, or productivity will remain low, exposing the tasks to the possibility of being exported to countries with a lower level of wages.

1.4   Prerequisites for studying computer science

Before deciding whether to enroll in higher studies in computer science, one might want to know what prerequisites would be necessary in order to do so.

Contrary to common belief, it is not necessary to know any programming language, nor is it necessary to know how to use widespread software on desktop computers. In fact, it is sometimes a disadvantage to know some programming already, because people who learn programming by themselves often acquire bad habits that constitute non-idiomatic use of a programming language, and such habits must be abandoned when more complex programs are to be written. Unfortunately, getting rid of such bad habits can be quite difficult, and in fact, it can even be psychologically difficult to admit that knowledge that has been acquired through considerable effort can be useless, or even counterproductive.

So what are the prerequisites? First of all, in order to be a good computer scientist, one has to be well organized. Programming in particular, but also algorithms and several other areas of computer science require the practitioner to manage vast amounts of information, and a large number of objects organized into complex structures. It must become a natural habit to take the time to organize all these objects such as files, subroutines, classes, modules, algorithms, etc., in order that these things be easy to find and retrieve. Certainly, being well organized is something that can be learned, but some people seem to have a natural tendency for this, and others seem to have a very hard time, despite years of experience.

Being well organized is important, but the practitioner must also have what is usually referred to as *intellectual curiosity*. Practicing any of the areas of computer science implies a life-long learning experience, simply because the domain is evolving so fast that knowledge might be obsolete only a few years after it was acquired, but also because the domain is so vast that even an advanced degree in computer science is not enough to master fully everything that is required to be effective and productive later on. It is therefore an absolute necessity for the practitioner to search systematically for information on how to solve problems, to read articles and books on a regular basis, to participate in continuing education, and to experiment with new tools and techniques. Without this intellectual curiosity, the level of knowledge will deteriorate *relative to that of recent graduates*, and relative to intellectually curious colleagues in only a few years.

1.5 Contents of this book

Even though computer science covers a large and growing number of areas, there are some aspects of the discipline that permeate each and every one of those areas. These aspects pretty much define what it means to be a computer scientist, so anyone who contemplates working in any of the areas mentioned in the previous section is very likely to use these aspects on a daily basis.

We think there are three such fundamental aspects of computer science. They are:

- Theory. To be able to make any kind of progress in any domain of computer science, it is necessary to develop a theory. Without theoretical results, there is no reason to believe that the practical methods developed to handle some situation will actually work. Theoretical results can also give insight into what kind of performance (execution time, memory use) can be expected from the methods.

- Algorithms. Any method in computer science involves designing a step-by-step solution to any instance of the problem, and this step-by-step solution must be formulated in such a way that a computer can execute it. The algorithms depend crucially on the theoretical results, and algorithms can be proven correct with respect to those results.

- Programming. Algorithms must be implemented using a *programming language* so that they can execute on a computer. A program is not just the simple translation of an algorithm into a programming language, because the program itself will need to deal with aspects such as understandability and maintainability. The choice of the programming language is crucial and depends on the area of interest, and sometimes it is even advantageous to design a so-called *domain-specific language* to solve the problem.

This books contains three parts, one part for each of the aspects listed above, but for a specific area, namely *graphs*. A graph is a mathematical object that turns out to be extraordinarily useful in many areas of computer science.

This first part of this book shows how to use *graph theory* to develop a collection of *theorems* about graphs. Those theorems will give us typical mathematical-style knowledge such as the conditions for the existence of some objects, but it will also give us hints related to the design of *algorithms* to find and manipulate those objects.

The second part of this book uses the theoretical results in the first part in order to develop a collection of *algorithms* and related *data structures*[2] that allow us to find and manipulate various graph-related objects.

The third part of this book shows how to implement the algorithms developed in the second part as a *program* in a particular programming language. This part of the book uses two different *abstract data types* which serve the purpose of keeping the final program understandable and maintainable. As we will show, different abstract data types will result in different programs, but they solve the same initial problem.

1.6   Choice of programming language

In order to write programs, it is necessary to use a *programming language*. There are many languages available. Many people think that these languages are essentially equivalent, but that is not the case. Each language has its advantages and disadvantages depending on what kind of programs it is used to write. To complicate the situation even further, some languages have several different *implementations*, each one with its own characteristics.

In order to choose a language or an implementation of a language for some programming task at hand, the developer must take into account several different

---

[2]A data structure is a potentially complex web of interconnected objects in the memory of a computer. We will have much more to say about this topic later in the book.

parameters for the languages to be considered:

- How fast the programs *execute*.

- How fast the programs are *compiled* (i.e., translated from the language into machine language).

- How *stable* the language or implementation is, i.e., whether the language or implementation has many defects.

- How expressive the language is.

- How easy it is to create *modular* programs using the language.

- What *programming paradigms* the language supports (imperative, functional, object-oriented, etc.).

- Whether it is easy or even possible to mix programs written in the language with programs written in other languages.

- Availability of libraries of functions, classes, etc.

- Portability of programs written in the language.

- Whether an international standard, independent of the supplier, exists for the language.

- Whether the implementation conforms to the available standard.

- Whether the language or implementation is likely to evolve to incorporate new features.

- Whether the *language* or *implementation* is likely to continue to exist in the future.

- Whether the *company supplying the language* or implementation is likely to continue to exist in the future.

- Whether several suppliers for the language exist.

- How easy the language is to *learn*.

- How easy the language is *to use for an experienced programmer*.

- How easy it is to find programmers who know the language.

Choosing a programming language for an introductory course in computer science is also tricky, but significantly less so than for the professional developer. The following considerations should be taken into account:

- Given the time available, the language should not be too hard to learn.

- It is advantageous to choose a language that is used for real applications, because then the student can take advantage of the knowledge of the language later.

- The language should allow the programmer to write *modular* and *understandable* programs.

A large number of considerations that are important to the professional developer are thus less important for a course, in particular whether the programs execute fast, and whether the language is likely to continue to exist in the future.

For this book, we have chosen a language named "Python". This language is available mainly as a single implementation in the form of *FLOSS* (Free, Libre, Open-Source Software). Choosing a language available this way for a course allows the students to install it and use it for free at home.

To give an idea of the characteristics of the language Python, we give a partial list of features[3]:

- Uniform reference semantics.

- Object-oriented programming with classes and class instances.

- Automatic memory management.

- Large number of libraries available.

- Easy to manipulate collections of objects.

---

[3]The reader is not expected to know the details of what these features mean, just to get an idea of the terminology that might be used to describe a programming language.

- Execution speed of programs is not fantastic.

- Block structure indicated by the use of *indentation*.

1.7 Why this books is self published

This book is not published the ordinary way through a publishing house. Instead it is *self published* though a company called CreateSpace, which is a member of the Amazon group. This way of publishing implies that the author makes available a PDF[4] file, which is then distributed to the Amazon company for sale to its customers. Instead of keeping a stock of already printed books, Amazon uses so-called *print on demand* technology so that a copy of the book is printed only when a customer has ordered it.

There are several advantages to publishing a book this way:

- The authors of a book may be convinced that the book represents a novelty on the market, perhaps because it has a different approach to some domain compared to existing books, even though to a publishing house, the book might just look like yet another book in an existing domain. Self publishing allows the authors to publish the book at no cost other than the investment of writing it.

- Self publishing allows the author a reasonable return on the investment of writing a book known to be *low volume*.

- Since there is no stock of already printed books, it is easy to publish *updated versions* of the book, at essentially no extra cost. We intend to take advantage of this possibility by publishing *corrections* to existing editions and *new editions* when a new material is added.

- The authors retain all rights to the material, which makes it easier to create derivative work such as translations, and to include parts of one book into other books by the same author.

---

[4]PDF means Portable Document Format. It is a file format invented by Adobe Systems, and with a specification that has been an open standard since 2008.

- We firmly believe that, above and beyond covering their cost for reproduction, storage, distribution, logistics, and advertising, traditional publishing houses take an unreasonable share of the profit that books generate. Self publishing is one way of reacting to the current state of affairs.

Self publishing also has some disadvantages of course:

- With self publishing, it is not possible to take advantage of the marketing machine of a publishing house. In particular, publishing houses distribute *catalogs* which feature their books.

- It is more prestigious to publish though a publishing house, in particular if it is a famous one, so there is not as much glory in self publishing.

1.8   Feedback and updates

The current version of this book is 2.0, which means that the major version number is 2 and the minor version number is 0. Major version 1 was published only in French. This version contains some significant modifications, improvements, and additions.

If you find any errors or omissions in this book, we would like to know about them. Send email to robert.strandh@gmail.com and we will get back to you as soon as we can. You can also send us email if you have any questions, or if you would like us to email you some of the code from this book.

We intend to make updates available on a regular basis, by publishing corrected minor versions. A new major version will be published as a result of major additions or modifications.

1.9   Organization of this book

This book is organized in three main parts plus appendices.

In the first part ("Foundation"), we introduce the mathematical object that is studied in this book, namely the *graph*. Here, we present several possible definitions of this object, and we analyze advantages and disadvantages of each definition. We also introduce a number of important concepts related to graphs.

In the second part ("Algorithms"), we discuss the concept of an *algorithm*. In this part, we also introduce the concept of *asymptotic worst-case complexity* which is an extremely useful concept for determining the *efficiency* of an algorithm, and for comparing two algorithms with respect to their efficiency.

In the third part ("Programming"), we explain why writing a program requires the programmer to follow certain elementary rules, and we then give a quick introduction to the language Python. We end this part by showing and analyzing a selection of programs on graphs.

Part I

Foundation

The foundations of computer science have a lot in common with *mathematics*. Computer science is a young discipline, so it is natural to borrow ideas from other disciplines. In particular, *mathematical notation* has evolved over centuries and is now an international language that is universally understood by practitioners of the domain. So when a computer scientist needs to be precise about the objects that are manipulated by computer programs, it is a good instinct to try to take advantage of the existing notation developed and used by mathematicians with such great success.

But there are some important differences between computer science and mathematics when it comes to the formalism that the two disciplines need. There are essentially two major differences.

First, the objects of computer science are often *mutable* meaning that they can change over time, whereas mathematical objects are typically *immutable*. When objects are mutable, and in particular when those objects are highly complex, *object identity* becomes an issue. Thus, in mathematics, there is typically no discussion about whether two object are *the same* or *different*, because to a mathematician, the answer is usually crystal clear. But with objects such as *genomes, viruses, illnesses, languages, sentiments*, etc., the identity is no longer so clear. Even with more concrete objects such as *books*, things get more complicated. Are two copies of "Introduction to Computer Science" *the same book* or *two different books*? If they are different, so that each individual copy has its own identity, then a concept such as "the books that stand next to it" is a uniquely determined idea, whereas in the second case, "the books that stand next to it" is a concept that requires us to supply another object such as a "book case" in order to make it precise. But a concept such as "the people who read it recently" does not require us to make a distinction between two different copies.

Second, mathematical notation is mostly meant to be read by humans, and humans are tolerant when it comes to approximations and misuse of language. Thus, mathematical notation can be less detailed than the notation required by a computer scientist, while still serving its purpose perfectly well, whereas if there are omissions in the notation used by a computer scientist, the computer will either reject it or give the wrong answer. Neither is acceptable. And even if the notation is not meant to be read directly by a computer, at some point, the computer scientist must turn the notation into a *computer program*, and then any lack of detail will create a conundrum that has to be resolved before work on the program can progress.

In this part of the book, we assume the consequences of the need for precision stated above, by being as precise as possible when it comes to our notation. Some readers might be unused to that level of precision, and so will find the notation verbose and tedious, and perhaps even scary. To help the reader, we try to systematically explain every concept, notation, definition, and theorem, not only with formal notation borrowed from mathematics, but we also examine in great detail what these items mean, often in several different ways, using plain English. And we try to point out reasons for a particular expression, and potential pitfalls when attempting to do it differently.

Chapter 2

The graph

In this chapter we introduce the main object discussed in this book, namely the *graph*.

2.1 Objects and relations between objects

Behind the concept of a graph is a *collection of objects* and a *binary relation* between those objects.

A *binary relation* is a *set of pairs* of objects. In mathematics, a relation is often expressed as a *predicate*, such as $<$ for the relation named *is strictly less than* or $=$ for the relation named *is equal to*. In mathematics, these relations are characterized by the fact that they apply to an *infinite* number of objects, for instance all real numbers. A relation $\mathcal{R}$ is thus an infinite set of pairs (x, y) such that $x\mathcal{R}y$. The set corresponding to the predicate $=$ is thus $\{(34.5, 34.5), (1/4, 0.25), \ldots\}$.

The set of real numbers is not only infinite, but in addition it is not *enumerable* or, more correctly, not *recursively enumerable*[1]. If a set is not recursively enumerable, it means that it is impossible to find a way to write down the

---

[1]The *rational numbers* are, however, recursively enumerable. One way of creating a list of them, is to write them down in increasing order of the *sum of the numerator and denominator*.

objects that it contains in the form of a list, even if an infinite list is allowed.

Even though a relation can contain arbitrary pairs of objects, some relations are more *structured* in that they obey some additional *restrictions* on what pairs they may contain:

- A relation may be *symmetric*, which means that if a pair (x, y) is in the relation, then so is the pair (y, x). An example of such a relation would be *share a common language*.

- A relation may be *antisymmetric*, which means that if a pair (x, y) such that $x \neq y$ is in the relation, then the pair (y, x) is *not* in the relation. An example of such a relation would be *is older than*.

- A relation may be *reflexive*, which means that for all objects x in the set, the pair (x, x) is in the relation. An example of such a relation would be *is at least as old as*.

- A relation may be *irreflexive*, which means that for all objects x in the set, the pair (x, x) is *not* in the relation. An example of such a relation would be *is older than*.

- A relation may be *transitive*, which means that if the pairs (x, y) and (y, z) are both in the relation, then so is the pair (x, z). Again, *is older than* is an example of such a relation.

Many other interesting restrictions are recognized and have been named. Some of them are *combinations* of other restrictions. Thus, for instance, a relation that is reflexive, symmetric, and transitive is known as an *equivalence relation*.

In computer science, the objects are often more concrete than in traditional mathematics. They might be (computer representations of) people, molecules, electronic components, cities, or receivers/transmitters for mobile telephony. Frequently, a set of such objects is *finite*, or at least *enumerable*, which greatly simplifies the operations we need to accomplish on these sets.

When a set is of objects is finite, a relation containing *pairs* of objects must also be finite. In other words, if the relation is seen as a set of pairs of objects, the relation is a finite set. To be more precise, if the finite set of objects has n objects, then the set of pairs in the relation can have at most n^2 pairs in it.

Examples:

1. The set of objects is the set of all people present at a particular dinner party, and the relation is the set of all pairs of people (p_1, p_2) such that p_1 is an ancestor of p_2. In this example, the relation is not *symmetric*, which means that if (p_1, p_2) is in the relation, then it is not necessarily the case that (p_2, p_1) is in the relation as well. In fact, in this case, it is even *antisymmetric* which means that if p_1 is an ancestor of p_2 then p_2 can not be an ancestor of p_1, and the relation is also *transitive* which means that if p_1 is an ancestor of p_2 and p_2 is an ancestor of p_3, then p_1 is an ancestor of p_3.

2. The set of objects is the set of all people present at a particular dinner party, and the relation is the set of all pairs of people (p_1, p_2) such that p_1 is a *parent* of p_2. In this example, the relation is antisymmetric but not transitive.

3. The set of objects is the set of all people present at a particular dinner party, and the relation is the set of all pairs of people (p_1, p_2) such that p_1 is a *cousin* of p_2. In this case, the relation is symmetric, because if p_1 is a cousin of p_2, then p_2 is also a cousin of p_1.

4. The set of objects is the set of all atoms of a molecule, and the relation is the set of pairs of atoms (a_1, a_2) such that a_1 and a_2 share at least one electron. This relation is symmetric, and also *reflexive* which means that an atom always shares at least one electron with itself.

5. The set of objects is the set of electronic components of some circuit, and the relation is all the pairs (c_1, c_2) such that c_1 is directly connected to c_2.

6. The set of objects is the set of all relay stations in a network of mobile telephone communication, and the relation is the set of all pairs (s_1, s_2) such that there is a direct communication link (microwave, cable, fiber, etc.) from s_1 to s_2.

In the rest of this book, we will most often restrict ourselves to symmetric relations on finite sets of objects.

2.2   Graphical representation of a relation

When a set is finite (and does not contain too many elements), it is possible to represent a relation on this set by a *drawing* or a *figure*. Such a representation is often useful in order for people to understand a problem better.

Most often, the objects of the set are drawn as *circles* and the pairs of the relation are drawn as *lines* or *curves* connecting the circles.

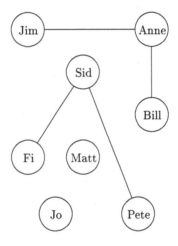

Figure 2.1: Cousins at a dinner party.

Figure 2.1 shows a representation of a graph in which the objects are the people present at a particular dinner party, and the relation is all the pairs representing cousins. In this example Jim and Anne are cousins, so are Anne and Bill, Sid and Fi, and Pete and Sid. Matt and Jo do not have any cousins present at this dinner party.

Notice that a figure like figure 2.1 can not express relations such as "ancestor" or "parent" discussed in section 2.1, because the two objects in a relation are not distinguishable. The two endpoints of a line segment are equivalent as far as the figure is concerned. In other words, the graph in this figure can illustrate only *symmetric* relations. Such a graph (i.e., a graph in which the relation shown is necessarily symmetric) is called an *undirected graph*. Since relations such as "ancestor" and "parent" are not symmetric, they can not be represented by a drawing such as the one in figure 2.1.

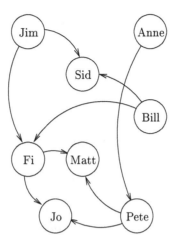

Figure 2.2: Parents at a dinner party.

Figure 2.2 shows a representation of a graph in which the objects are again the people present at some dinner party. This time, the relation contains all the pairs (p_1, p_2) such that p_1 is a *parent* of p_2. To distinguish two people participating in the relation, we draw an *arrow* pointing to p_1. In this example, Bill and Jim are the sons of Fi and Sid, Anne is the daughter of Pete (Anne's mother is not present). Jo and Matt are the parents of Fi and Pete, and are thus grandparents of Bill, Jim, and Anne. A graph of this type (in which the relation is not symmetric) is called a *directed graph* or a *digraph*.

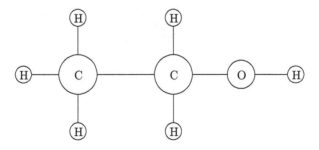

Figure 2.3: A molecule represented as a graph.

Figure 2.3 shows a graph that represents an organic molecule. In order to illustrate the different types of atoms, we have drawn the objects of the set using circles of different sizes, and we have marked each object with the corresponding chemical symbol.

2.3   Exercises

Exercise 2.1. *Draw an* undirected *graph representing the members of your family (brothers, sisters, uncles, aunts, cousins, children, etc.) and show the relation named* "age difference is less than 10 years".

Exercise 2.2. *Draw a* directed *graph representing the members of your family (brothers, sisters, uncles, aunts, cousins, children, etc.) and show the relation named* "is older than".

Exercise 2.3. *Draw a graph representing the states of the USA, and show the relation named* "share a border". *Should this graph be directed or undirected?*

Exercise 2.4. *Draw a graph representing the main rivers of the USA, together with the relation* "flow though the same state".

Exercise 2.5. *Draw a graph representing the countries in the European Union, together with the relation* "have a common official language".

Chapter 3

Concepts and notation

In this chapter, we introduce a certain number of *concepts* and some *notation* that may not be known to the reader. By a *concept*, we mean a *name* for some entity that has not previously been named. By *notation*, we mean one or more symbols to which we attribute some special meaning.

Most of the time, these concepts and this notation seem more complicated than they really are. But there are several reasons to introduce them:

- We avoid repeating the same long phrase over and over again each time we want to talk about the concept.

- A concept and notation allow us to be more precise than if we use a phrase, because phrases are more ambiguous.

- Concepts and notation turn into an international language, because they replace a phrase in a particular natural language by something much simpler.

Let us take some examples well known to most readers:

1. The *square root* of a non-negative number x is a non-negative number such that when multiplied by itself, the result is exactly x. The notation

for this concept is $\sqrt{x}$. Suppose we would like to express that $\sqrt{x} = \frac{x}{\sqrt{x}}$, but we do not have the right to use the notation $\sqrt{x}$, nor the concept *square root*. We would obtain a phrase like "the non-negative number such that when multiplied by itself yields the non-negative number x, is equal to x divided by the non-negative number such that when multiplied by itself yields the non-negative number x".

2. The functions $sin\ \alpha$ and $cos\ \alpha$ are defined with respect to a unit circle with its center in the origin of a 2-dimensional coordinate system and a ray through the origin. In order to express a relation such as $sin^2\ \alpha + cos^2\ \alpha = 1$ without using neither the concept of *sine* and *cosine*, nor the notation $sin\ \alpha$ or $cos\ \alpha$, one would need a phrase so long that it would be totally incomprehensible.

Introducing new concepts and new notation is thus both normal and quite desirable. In this book, we try to choose those concepts and that notation with great care, for several reasons:

- We have to introduce concepts and notation for objects that are unknown to the reader because the *domain of discourse* is new (the graph).

- In computer science, it is common to introduce a new concept or some new notation to be used only in a chapter of a book or in a scientific article, whereas most concepts of mathematics have been standardized for a long time.

- Also in computer science, there are variations concerning many concepts and some notation according to the author of the book or article.

- In computer science, the objects manipulated are more complex and more concrete than those habitually manipulated in mathematics. It is therefore important to be careful when introducing new concepts and new notation so as to make sure that the right objects are meant.

When a new concept is introduced, it would be *possible* to use some nonsense word for it, so for instance instead of calling the main object of interest in this book a *graph*, we could have called it (say) a "blinchpan". This is not often the method chosen. Instead, existing words are reused. It is important to realize that the meaning of this word in the ordinary language frequently has very little to do with the concept it was chosen to name. For instance:

- The word *graph* suggests some kind of picture or diagram, but in fact as it is used in this book, it is just two sets and a function.

- Mathematics has a long history of reusing common words, so it is important to realize that there is nothing *natural* about the natural numbers, and the *real* numbers are no more real than the *imaginary* numbers.

- Just because the adjective *simple* is used to qualify some concept (simple graph, simple rewrite system, etc), one should not expect those objects to be simple in any traditional meaning of the word.

The reader can no doubt come up with many more examples where such everyday words are used differently in specific domains.

Getting used to this way of using existing words from the language may take some time, but it is nevertheless an important goal to anyone interested in studying computer science.

3.1 Concepts and notation related to sets

We will often use the concept of a *set* that we assume the reader is familiar with. However, there is a complicating factor about sets in computer science, namely that it is imperative to specify the *equality function*, i.e., how to determine whether two objects are *the same*.

Suppose that object a is a Volkswagen Polo registered in Belgium with a license plate of CTD-941, that object b is a Volkswagen Golf registered also in Belgium with a license plate of ABC-123, and that object c is a Volkswagen Polo registered in the Netherlands. Let us study the set $S = \{a, b\}$. Is c in this set? The answer depends on the equality function used. In an application that does not need to distinguish individual objects, but only different models, it is fair to say that $a = c$, and so c is in the set S. If the equality function used does not distinguish between the different models from the same company, then in fact S only contains a single element.

We use the notation $x \in S$ to mean that x is an element of the set S. This notation does not specify which equality function is used, so that must be mentioned explicitly, unless it is understood by context.

In order to talk about the *number of elements* of some set S, we use the notation $|S|$. The number of elements of a set is also called the *cardinality* of the set.

When some set S is a *subset* of some other set T, i.e., every element of S is also an element of T, we use the notation $S \subseteq T$, and it is possible that $S = T$. If we mean that S is a subset of T, but they *can not be the same set*, i.e., the set T contains at least one object that is not in S, then we use the notation $S \subset T$.

We frequently need to talk about all possible subsets of a set. For instance, suppose we have a set V containing three people: Anne, Jo, and Frank, so that $V = \{\text{Anne}, \text{Jo}, \text{Frank}\}$. We need a concept in order to talk about the set of all subsets of V, i.e., the set of the sets $\{\}$, $\{\text{Anne}\}$, $\{\text{Jo}\}$, $\{\text{Frank}\}$, $\{\text{Anne}, \text{Jo}\}$, $\{\text{Anne}, \text{Frank}\}$, $\{\text{Jo}, \text{Frank}\}$, and $\{\text{Anne}, \text{Jo}, \text{Frank}\}$. We call it the *powerset* of V, and the notation for it is $\mathcal{P}(V)$.

Occasionally, we need to use some notation for all the elements of a set except for some of them that are *excluded*. This concept is called *set difference*. The notation that means "the set of all the elements that are members of the set A except the elements that are members of the set B" is $A \setminus B$. When we want to exclude a single element x from A, we write $A \setminus \{x\}$.

3.2   Functions

A function is a mathematical object that, given an element of some set, yields an element of some other set. The reader is likely familiar with functions such as $y = sin\ \alpha$ which for an angle yields a coordinate. But it is possible to define functions on objects other than numbers. One might, for instance, imagine a function that, given a person, gives the date of birth of that person. We say that the function is *applied* to an *argument* and *returns* a *value*. In the case of $y = sin\ \alpha$, the argument is an angle and the value returned is a real number between -1 and 1. In the second example, the argument is a person and the return value is a date.

The set of all possible arguments to a function ϕ is the *domain* of the function, written $dom(\phi)$. The set of all possible values of a function is the *range* of the function, written $ran(\phi)$. The notation $\phi : dom(\phi) \longrightarrow ran(\phi)$ is frequently used. For instance, for the sine function we have $sin : \mathbb{R} \longrightarrow [-1, 1]$.

Sometimes it is not practical to give the range of a function, perhaps because it would require enumerating all possible values. In that case, one can use a *superset* of the range that is more practical to give. Such a superset is called the *codomain* of the function. Take for instance the function *isqr* that for any integer n, computes n^2. The *range* of the *isqr* function is $\{0, 1, 4, 9, \ldots\}$ but one can write $isqr : \mathbb{Z} \longrightarrow \mathbb{N}$ even though most elements of $\mathbb{N}$ are *not* in the range of the function *isqr*. Here $\mathbb{N}$ is the codomain of the function, and it is not unique.

To show a *particular* function that can be expressed in mathematical notation, we use an arrow like this: $\mapsto$ (pronounced "maps to"), where to the left of the arrow we show the *arguments* to the function, and to the right of the arrow we show an expression that determines its value as a function of the arguments. So for instance, the notation $x, y \mapsto 2x + y^2$ means a function of two arguments which returns two times the first argument plus the second argument squared.

3.3   Terminology of logic

In order to understand a theorem or a proof, it is necessary to understand certain concepts and some notation of logic.

When we say that "A is a necessary condition for B", it means "in order for B to be true, A must be true". For instance, "the expiration date of the credit card is in the future" is a necessary condition for "the credit card is valid". In other words, in order for the credit card to be valid, the expiration date must be in the future. If the credit card is valid, w can conclude that the expiration date is in the future. Another way of expressing the phrase "A is a necessary condition for B" is "B implies A" which is written $B \Rightarrow A$. It is *not* possible to conclude that $A \Rightarrow B$. It is not just because the expiration date of the credit card is in the future that the card is necessarily valid. There may be other conditions for it to be valid, such as nobody having blocked it because it was lost or stolen.

When we say "A is a sufficient condition for B", it is equivalent to "A implies B" written $A \Rightarrow B$. An example would be "Jim is carrying an umbrella" is a sufficient condition for "Jim does not get wet when it rains".

But the phrases "A is a necessary condition for B" and "A is a sufficient condition for B" also have an interpretation other than purely logic. They also express an objective. The objective of both the phrases above is B, and we use A to verify whether the objective is obtained. In the case of the phrase "A is a necessary condition for B", we can check whether by any chance A is *false*, in which case B is also false. So if the expiration date of the card is in the past, the card is not valid. In the case of the phrase "A is a sufficient condition for B", we can check whether A by any chance is *true* in which case B is true as well. If Jim is carrying an umbrella, then he does not get wet when it rains. Even though the phrase "A is a necessary condition for B" is logically equivalent to the phrase "B is a sufficient condition for A", it is unusual to make use of this equivalence. We do not say "the credit card is valid" is a sufficient condition for "the expiration date is in the future", because this phrase expresses the objective that the expiration date be in the future, and in order to check that, we wish to check the validity of the card. Similarly, we do not start by checking whether Jim got wet when it rained, in order to determine whether Jim might be carrying an umbrella.

Another way of expressing "A is a necessary condition for B" is "B only if A" as in "the card is valid only if the expiration date is in the future". Similarly, "A is a sufficient condition for B" can be expressed as "B if A", as in "Jim does not get wet when it rains if he carries an umbrella". These phrases clearly express the desired objectives. We do not say "Jim carries an umbrella only if he does not get wet when it rains".

Frequently, a condition (or a combination of conditions) A may be both necessary and sufficient for some other condition B. In that case, we can say "A if and only if B" (often abbreviated "A iff B"). For instance, "A storm is considered to be a hurricane if and only if it has a force of at least 12 on the Beaufort scale". This type of phrase is often used to define a new concept, here "hurricane". Even though the phrase "A if and only if B" is logically equivalent to "B if and only if A", for the same reasons as above, they are rarely used that way. In a phrase of the type "A if and only if B", A is the concept to be defined.

In order to prove a theorem, we often use a technique called *proof by contradiction*. When using this technique, we need to compute the negation of a phrase.

In order to do that, it is important to know the form of the negation of a certain number of common phrases of logic. Given a phrase A, the negation of A is written $\neg A$. The negation of the phrase "A only if B" is "not B but A", as in "the expiration date of the card is in the past, but the card is valid". From the point of view of logic reasoning, "but" means "and", so we can express the same thing as "the expiration date of the card is in the past, and the card is valid". In order to see this, it is important to to realize that from the point of view of logic, the phrase "A only if B" is the same thing as $A \Rightarrow B$, which is the same as B *or* $\neg A$. The negation of B *or* $\neg A$ is $\neg B$ *and* A.

Similarly, the negation of the phrase "A if B" is "B but not A" as in "Jim was carrying an umbrella, but he still got wet when it rained". From the point of view of logic, this phrase is the same as B *and* $\neg A$.

If a phrase contains quantifiers such as $\forall a\ A$ or $\exists b\ B$, computing the negation is a bit harder. The negation of the phrase $\forall a\ A$ is $\exists a\ \neg A$. For instance, the negation of the phrase "all prime numbers are odd" is "there exists a prime number that is not odd", or "there exists a prime number that is even".

The negation of the phrase $\exists b\ B$ is $\forall b\ \neg B$. For instance, the negation of the phrase "there exists a non-nearsighted person" is "all persons are nearsighted"

3.4   Theorems and proofs

As we have pointed out already, computer science is a young discipline with many things in common with a much older discipline, namely mathematics. There is one aspect that these two disciplines have in common, and which distinguishes them from the *sciences* (physics, chemistry, etc.). The sciences study the *real world*, by *observing* it, then making *models* about how it works in order to *make predictions* about it, which are finally *validated by experiments*. Computer science and mathematics both have the distinguished luxury of making up their own worlds. The objects that are studied in computer science and mathematics are imaginary, and the laws that govern them are a direct consequence of how the objects were *defined*. The objects can still be complex, though, and behave in surprising ways, so we still need to *observe* them. We can even experiment with them, but an experiment is not the ultimate validation of a hypothesis about an object. Instead, we use *theorems* and *proofs* to validate hypotheses.

The reader might already have been exposed to theorems and proofs of mathematics. Often they are presented in a way that makes them seem non-obvious. The reader is often left with a bitter taste in his or her mouth, and with many questions unanswered, such as:

- Why is it important to prove this theorem? The answer often is that the result is needed at some later point to prove something more important, but the reader is left to guess when this point will come.

- How did this proof come about?

- Is this the best way, or perhaps the only way to prove the theorem? How can I be sure?

- What makes this "proof" a real proof?

Let us answer the last question right away: A proof is a real proof when both the author and the reader are convinced that it is true. Most such proofs rely at least partly on natural language, and the reader has a tendency to "fill in the blanks". While this tendency simplifies both writing and reading proofs, unfortunately it also makes it more likely that proofs contain errors, and that these errors remain undetected by the reader.

There is a common misconception that proofs in mathematics and computer science are infallible. They are not, and incorrect "proofs" in published articles are regularly discovered. Typically, someone discovers a counterexample to the theorem, which then both shows that the "proof" was incorrect, and often also provides an indication as to how to weaken the statement of the theorem to make it true.

Theorems and proofs are even more important in computer science than in mathematics. A computer scientist uses theorems and proofs in order to be *convinced* that a particular computer program will work. Without these tools, the computer scientist will always be left with a doubt as to whether the program really works. Sometimes, the program in fact *does not* work, and in some cases the consequences might be disastrous such as when the program controls a nuclear power plant or a flying airplane.

This book contains some theorems and some proofs. We attempt to make sure the reader understands the reason for their existence, and we attempt to make sure that the reader gets an idea of how the theorems and the proofs came about.

There are only a handful of different *proof patterns*; i.e., proofs fall into *categories*, and all proofs in a category resemble one another in that they have the same basic structure. In this book, we use only two such proof patterns. One is called *proof by induction* and the other is called *proof by contradiction*. In this section, we describe the two, and also show examples of theorems that lend themselves to each kind of proof.

3.4.1   Proof by induction

Let us start with *proof by induction*, and with a theorem that the reader has very likely already come across. The theorem tells us a closed formula for an *arithmetic series*, i.e, a sum of numbers where two consecutive numbers always have the same *difference*.

In an attempt to make the reader understand how proofs of this kind come about, we will develop the proof in the same order as a typical mathematician would do.

There is an anecdote about the great mathematician Carl Friedrich Gauss that claims that when he was young, as a punishment he was given the task by his teacher to compute the sum of the integers from 1 to 100. Young Gauss is said to have produced the answer in seconds.

Let us try to follow the possible reasoning of young Gauss, and then generalize that reasoning into a theorem and a proof.

If we are asked to produce the value of the sum $s = 1 + 2 + \ldots + 100$, we might realize that if we take $1 + 100$, then $2 + 99$, etc., each such term has the same value, namely 101. Thus we get $s = (1 + 100) + (2 + 99) + \ldots + (50 + 51)$, or

$s = 101 + 101 + \ldots + 101$. How many terms are there? We are lucky because in the original sum, there was an even number (100) of terms, so when we group them together, we get half as many, in this case 50. So the answer is that $s = 101 \cdot 50 = 5050$. So far, so good.

A mathematician that sees that result will probably immediately contemplate what the answer would be if we were asked to compute $s = 1 + 2 + \ldots + 102$, or even $s = 1 + 2 + \ldots + n$ for any *even* value of n. This computation is not hard. We can use the same method as before. Clearly, the individual terms become $1 + n$, $2 + (n-1)$, etc., so that each such term has the value $1 + n$. How many terms are there? The answer is $n/2$, because we grouped the original together in pairs. It then appears that $s = 1 + 2 + \ldots + n = n(n+1)/2$ for even values of n.

The first thing to do at this point would be to do a *test*. We already know that $1 + 2 + \ldots + 100 = 5050$, so it had better be true that $n(n+1)/2 = 5050$ when $n = 100$ or else we have made a mistake. Luckily, this is the case, so we feel a bit more confident. In this day and age, as computer scientists, we now typically use a method that was not available to young Gauss: we write a computer program that will take a number n and compute two things, namely the sum $s = 1 + 2 + \ldots + n$ and $n(n+1)/2$ and compare the two. Then we execute that program for a large number of values of n, such as $n = 2, 4, 6, \ldots, 10000$. If the program confirms that the two values computed are the same for that many n, we feel a little more certain again.

The next step might be to attempt to see what happens when n is *odd*. Let us start with $n = 99$. Now we get $(1 + 99) + (2 + 98) + \ldots + (49 + 51) + 50$. It seems that we get 49 terms with a value of 100 and one term with the value of 50. Generalizing, we guess that it might be that $1 + 2 + \ldots + n = (n-1)/2 \cdot (n+1) + (n+1)/2$. With some simple algebra we can simplify this expression so that $(n-1)/2 \cdot (n+1) + (n+1)/2 = (n+1)(n-1+1)/2 = n(n+1)/2$. Eureka! It appears that we have the same result whether n is even or odd. The computer program is quickly generalized to test odd numbers as well, and we again feel more confident.

We feel so confident that we can start formulating a *theorem*:

Theorem 3.1. $\forall n \in \mathbb{N}, \sum_{i=1}^{n} i = n(n+1)/2$

We strongly feel that theorem 3.1 is true, and we have tested it for many values of n, but how can we be *sure*? The trick is the following:

1. Show that the theorem is valid for some small value(s) of n.

2. Show that IF the theorem is valid for $n = 1, n = 2, \ldots, n = a$ for ANY value of a (we are not saying it IS valid, only "IF THAT HAPPENS TO BE THE CASE"), THEN it is ALSO valid for $n = a + 1$.

If we can do both those things, we can use item number 1 in the list to show that it is true for (say) $n = 1$. Then we can use item number 2 in the list to show that it is also true for $n = 2$, so that it is true for $n = 1$, and $n = 2$. Then we can use item 2 in the list again, to show that it is also true for $n = 3$, so that it is true for $n = 1$, $n = 2$, and $n = 3$, etc.

Mathematicians convinced themselves a long time ago that this kind of reasoning is valid, so whenever it is used, it is considered legitimate. This kind of reasoning is know as *mathematical induction*, and a proof that uses this technique is called a *proof by induction*.

Let us see how this applies to theorem 3.1. Clearly, the theorem is true when $n = 1$. What if it were true for $n = 1, n = 2, \ldots n = a$? Then is it also true for $n = a + 1$? To make things easier, let us say that $b = a + 1$. Now if we have a sum like $\sum_{i=1}^{b} i$, we can write it as $\sum_{i=1}^{a+1} i$ which is the same as $\sum_{i=1}^{a} i + (a + 1)$. But we have assumed that $\sum_{i=1}^{a} i = a(a + 1)/2$, so that $\sum_{i=1}^{b} i = \sum_{i=1}^{a} i + (a + 1) = a(a + 1)/2 + (a + 1)$ which can be simplified to $a^2/2 + a/2 + a + 1 = a^2/2 + 3a/2 + 1$. Our hope is that this will turn out to be the same thing as $b(b + 1)/2$. But $b = a + 1$, so $b(b + 1)/2 = (a + 1)(a + 2)/2$ which is $a^2/2 + 3a/2 + 1$! Eureka again!

Formally, this is how a proof by induction of theorem 3.1 would be written:

Proof. (of theorem 3.1)

By induction on n.

(base case) The theorem is trivially true for $n = 1$.

(induction hypothesis) Suppose that $\sum_{i=1}^{n} i = n(n + 1)/2$ for every $n \in \mathbb{N}$ such that $n \leq k$.

(induction step) We show that $\sum_{i=1}^{n} i = n(n+1)/2$ for $n = (k+1)$ as follows: $\sum_{i=1}^{(k+1)} i = \sum_{i=1}^{k} i + (k+1)$. By induction hypothesis $\sum_{i=1}^{k} i = k(k+1)/2$. Thus, $\sum_{i=1}^{(k+1)} i = \sum_{i=1}^{k} i + (k+1) = k(k+1)/2 + (k+1) = k(k+1)/2 + 2(k+1)/2 = (k(k+1) + 2(k+1))/2 = (k+2)(k+1)/2 = (k+1)(k+2)/2$. It follows that $\sum_{i=1}^{n} i = n(n+1)/2$ for $n = (k+1)$. □

The main difficulty with coming up with a proof by induction is to find some quantity on which to base the induction. In the case of the proof above, the induction was on n, i.e., the last number of the term. With theorems about integers, it is usually not too hard to come up with this quantity. When the theorems involve more complex objects, such as graphs, then it can be harder. Frequently, we have to come up with some concept of *size* of the object to base the induction on.

A minor difficulty is to find the value of the quantity for the base case. It is considered more elegant to use a smaller value, and it is frowned upon to use a value larger than what is necessary, especially if it complicates the verification of the base case.

3.4.2   Proof by contradiction

The second kind of proof used in this book falls in the category called *proof by contradiction*. It is frequently used to prove theorems of the form $A \Rightarrow B$.

The proof works by supposing the *opposite* of what we want to prove, and then showing by a series of logical steps that we obtain a logical contradiction. Mathematicians have long ago convinced themselves that when a logical contradiction is obtained, there is something wrong in the premises. In a proof by contradiction, this conviction translates to the supposition being false. Since the supposition was the opposite of what we wanted to prove, and it is false, then what we wanted to prove must be true. That way, the proof is complete.

If the theorem is of the form $A \Rightarrow B$, as we have seen in section 3.3, it is logically the same as B *or* $\neg A$. The negation of B *or* $\neg A$ is $\neg B$ *and* A.

Perhaps the most famous proof by contradiction is this one:

Theorem 3.2. $\sqrt{2}$ *is not a rational number.*

Let is try to put this theorem in the form $A \Rightarrow B$. To do that, let us first make sure we understand what we mean by the phrase "the positive number x is rational". Mathematically, it means $\exists a, b \in \mathbb{N}$ such that $x = a/b$. Thus, "the positive number x is NOT rational" means $\nexists a, b \in \mathbb{N}$ such that $x = a/b$.

Now we can express "$\sqrt{2}$ is not a rational number" as "$x^2 = 2 \Rightarrow \nexists a, b \in \mathbb{N}$ such that $x = a/b$". To make a proof by contradiction, we now need to negate that phrase, so we obtain "$\sqrt{2}$ is a rational number" which gives "$x^2 = 2$ *and* $\exists a, b \in \mathbb{N}$ such that $x = a/b$". We can also see this by using what was said in section 3.3, so that we need to obtain "$\neg B$ *and* A" where B is "$\nexists a, b \in \mathbb{N}$ such that $x = a/b$" and A is "$x^2 = 2$". The proof below shows that this phrase leads to a contradiction.

Of course, in addition to negating logical statements, and deriving conclusions from that, every proof also invokes some knowledge which is specific to the domain (in this case about natural numbers). The main difficulty in finding a proof for a theorem is to find exactly what domain-specific knowledge to use in order to obtain a contradiction.

Here is the formal proof of theorem 3.2:

Proof. (of theorem 3.2)

Suppose $\sqrt{2}$ is a rational number. Then it can be expressed as $\sqrt{2} = a/b$ with $a, b \in \mathbb{N}$. In fact, we can choose a and b so that they have no common factors. If they happen to have a common factor (say f), then divide by f so that we obtain $a' = a/f$ and $b' = b/f$, and consider a'/b' instead of a/b, and continue until they have no common factors. Next compute the square of each side of this equation, giving $2 = a^2/b^2$ and then $a^2 = 2b^2$. This means that a^2 is even, so that a is even as well. We can therefore express a as $2c$, where $c \in \mathbb{N}$. Now since $a^2 = 2b^2$ we also have $(2c)^2 = 2b^2$ or $4c^2 = 2b^2$ and then $2c^2 = b^2$. This means that b^2 is even so that b is even as well. But now, both a and b are even, so they have a factor 2 in common. Since we have made sure that a and b did not have any common factors, we now have a contradiction. Therefore, it must be the case that our assumption was false, namely that $\sqrt{2}$ is a rational number. Therefore $\sqrt{2}$ is *not* a rational number. $\square$

There are a few pieces of domain-specific knowledge invoked here:

- It is always possible to *canonicalize* a rational number a/b so that a and b have no common factors.

- If the square of some natural number n is even, then n itself is also even.

3.5   Exercises

Exercise 3.1. *Express the relation $\sin^2 \alpha + \cos^2 \alpha = 1$ without using the names of the function sin and cos.*

Exercise 3.2. *Given the set {Linux, Windows, MacOS}. What is its powerset?*

Exercise 3.3. *What is the cardinality of the powerset of a set of size n? Hint : each element is either a member or not a member of one of the sets.*

Exercise 3.4. *What is the domain of the function $x \mapsto 1/x$?*

Exercise 3.5. *What is the domain of the function $\alpha \mapsto \sin \alpha$? What is its range? Is it possible to imagine several different answers to these questions? If so, which?*

Exercise 3.6. *What is the domain of the function "how many wheels"? Is it possible to imagine several possibilities?*

Exercise 3.7. *If the domain of the function "number of counties" is the set of states of the USA, what is its range?*

Chapter 4

Definitions of a graph

In this chapter, we examine some different possible definitions of a graph. Choosing the right definition for an application is important, because the usefulness of the application may depend on it.

4.1 Main definition

Here is the definition that we use in the remainder of this book:

Definition 4.1. *A graph is a triple* (V, E, ϕ)*, where* V *is a set of elements called the* vertices *of the graph,* E *is a set of elements called the* edges *of the graph, and* ϕ *is a function* $\phi : E \longrightarrow \mathcal{P}(V)$ *such that* $\forall e \in E, |\phi(e)| \in \{1, 2\}$.

Let us examine in detail what definition 4.1 means.

First of all, definition 4.1 says that a graph is a *triple*. This means that the names V, E and ϕ are of no importance. These names exist only so that they can be referred to later on in the definition. Instead, when we say that "A graph is a triple", we mean that "A graph is an object with three ordered components".

The remainder of definition 4.1 explains the nature of each component of the triple.

Concerning the explanation of the *first* component of the triple, definition 4.1 gives us very little information about its nature. We learn that it is a *set*, and we are advised that if anyone ever uses a phrase such as "the vertices of G", then they refer to the elements of the set in the first component of the triple G. But definition 4.1 gives us great liberty concerning the nature of these vertices, because it does not restrict them in any way.

With the second component of the triple, it is the same thing as with the first component. Again, definition 4.1 says very little about its nature. Like the first component of the triple, the second one is also a *set*. The only difference between the first and the second components is that we are advised that if anyone ever uses a phrase such as "the edges of G", then they refer to the elements of the set in the second component of the triple G.

The main information in definition 4.1 lies in the explanation of the *third* component of the triple. Definition 4.1 says that this component of the triple is a *function*.

The notation $\phi : E \longrightarrow \ldots$ says that the *domain* of the function (See section 3.2.) is whatever is in the second component of the triple. In other words, the function of the third component of the triple must be a function of a single argument, and that single argument must be one of the elements of the set in the second component of the triple (i.e., an *edge*).

Definition 4.1 also tells us about the *codomain* (See section 3.2.) of the function in the third component of the triple. The notation $\phi : \ldots \longrightarrow \mathcal{P}(V)$ says that "the codomain of the function is the powerset of the set that is in the first component of the triple". (The concept of a *powerset* is explained in section 3.1). This means that a value returned by the function in the third component is a set, and such a set contains some of the objects that are also elements of the set in the first component of the triple. Using the word "vertices" for the elements of the set of the first component of the triple, we can say that "a value returned by the function is a set of vertices".

Finally, definition 4.1 gives us a *restriction* concerning the nature of the sets that can be values of the function in the third component of the triple. It says that $\forall e \in E, |\phi(e)| \in \{1, 2\}$. We can translate this formula to "no matter what (valid) argument you give to the function in the third triple of the component, the set that it returns contains either a single element or two elements". Using the words *vertices*, and *edges* the way the definition advises us to do, we can say "the function maps an edge to a set of either one or two vertices". An edge that maps to a single vertex is called a *loop*.

When we know the names of the components of a graph, as when we say "given a graph $G = (V, E, \phi)$", we use these names to refer to them later, as in V when we mean "the vertices of G", E when we mean the "the edges of G", and ϕ to mean "the function that is the third component of G". When we do *not* know the names of the components, as when we just say "given a graph G", then we use the notation $V(G)$ to mean "the vertices of G", $E(G)$ when we mean the "the edges of G", and $\phi(G)$ to mean "the function that is the third component of G".

4.2   Consequences of main definition

At this point, the reader has probably already made the connection between (on the one hand) the vertices and edges of definition 4.1 and (on the other hand) the circles and line segments of figure 2.1 of chapter 2. But before doing that, it might be wise to convince ourselves that the objects mentioned in definition 4.1 can be of any nature, not just circles and line segments.

So for instance let us consider the following object:
$(\{1, 2, 3, 4, 6, 9\}, \{1, 2, 3\}, x \mapsto \{2x, x^2\})$.

Let us make sure that this example object is really a graph according to definition 4.1. Clearly, it is a triple. Clearly, the first and second components of the triple are sets. It might be surprising to the reader that the elements of both those sets are positive integers. But there is nothing in definition 4.1 that prevents that. Definition 4.1 just advices us that 1, 2, 3, 4, 6, and 9 can be referred to as *vertices* and that 1, 2, and 3 can be referred to as *edges*. The fact that 1 and 2 are both vertices and edges also does not pose a problem because there is nothing in definition 4.1 that requires those sets to be disjoint.

Continuing with that example, now that we have convinced ourselves that the first and second components of the triple conform to definition 4.1, we examine the third component, i.e, the *function*. The notation $x \mapsto \{2x, x^2\})$ means that for an argument x to the function, the value is a set containing the numbers $2x$ and x^2. So the value is a set which it is supposed to be according to definition 4.1, and the set contains either 2 elements (if $2x$ and x^2 are different) or 1 element (if they are the same). So far, so good. Now, it only remains to verify that the possible values of the function (i.e. its *range*, see section 3.2) are indeed sets of elements of the first component of the triple. The only method is to enumerate the values of the function for all possible arguments, so here we go: $1 \mapsto \{2,1\}$, $2 \mapsto \{4,4\} = \{4\}$, and $3 \mapsto \{6,9\}$. A quick check tells us that 2, 1, 4, 6, and 9 are all elements of the set of the first component of the triple.

We can conclude that $(\{1,2,3,4,6,9\}, \{1,2,3\}, x \mapsto \{2x, x^2\})$ is indeed a graph according to definition 4.1.

In the preceding paragraphs, we have seen that definition 4.1 gives us great liberty when it comes to the nature of the objects that make up a graph. However, we are typically going to use graphs to represent relations between more concrete objects.

In fact, the graphs that are typically treated by computer scientists have the following characteristics:

- The set of vertices is finite.

- The set of edges is finite.

- The set of vertices and the set of edges are disjoint.

- Vertices are objects that represent real objects such as people, automobiles, cities, or more abstract objects such as feelings and illnesses.

- The set of edges represents a real relation between the vertices such as "*are cousins*", "*have almost the same fuel efficiency*", "*have a direct flight between them*", or "*have at least one symptom in common*".

- The function ϕ can not be expressed by a simple formula, and can only be expressed by a complete enumeration of the value for each argument.

When these restrictions apply, and when in addition the set of vertices and the set of edges both contain relatively few elements, then illustrating the graph in the form of a *drawing* or a *figure* is a good way of presenting it. As illustrated by figure 2.3, additional information can be conveyed in such a drawing, and the additional information may improve the presentation.

4.3 Relation between main definition and a program

It is often desirable to give a more concrete interpretation of the definition of some object such as a *graph*. Here, we frequently give a parallel between a definition and a computer program. Definition 4.1 will then be interpreted like this:

> In a program that manipulates graphs, given an object of type *graph*, we can obtain the set of vertices of the graph and the set of edges of the graph. Furthermore, given an edge of the graph, we can obtain the vertices (or vertex, in the case of a loop) incident to the edge by applying the function ϕ to the edge.

We suppose that these operations, that we call *primitive operations* are very fast, i.e., that the time to execute them is very short. The set of all primitive operations on an object, here a graph, is often called an *abstract data type*. Later in this book, we examine how to write programs by using abstract data types. At the moment, we simply observe that some operations are easy (i.e., fast, with a short execution time) and others are hard (i.e., slow) according to the abstract data type that is used. With definition 4.1 it is for instance easy to count the number of edges of the graph, but it is hard to find all the edges that are incident to a given vertex.

4.4 Alternative definition

There are other ways of defining a graph. Definition 4.2 is an example.

Definition 4.2. *(This is not the definition we use later in this book.)*
A graph is a triple (V, E, ψ), where V is a set of elements called the vertices *of the graph, E is a set of elements called the* edges *of the graph, and ψ is a function $\psi : V \longrightarrow \mathcal{P}(E)$ such that $\forall e \in E, |\{v \in V, \ e \in \psi(v)\}| \in \{1, 2\}$.*

While definition 4.2 is entirely equivalent to 4.1 in that it generates the same objects, the role of the function ψ is totally different from that of the function ϕ of definition 4.1. In definition 4.2, the domain of the function ψ is the set of *vertices* and its codomain is the *powerset of the set of edges*. Given a vertex v, the function ψ gives the set of edges incident to v. The restriction on the size of the set guarantees that an edge is present either in a single (in the case of a loop) or in two of these sets.

In the second part of this book, we show how to translate definitions 4.1 and 4.2 into *abstract data types*.

4.5   Exercises

Exercise 4.1. *Convince yourself that the following object is a graph according to definition 4.1:* $(\mathbb{R}, \mathbb{N}, x \mapsto \{e^x, \sin x\})$.

Chapter 5

Some properties of graphs

In this chapter, we examine some useful properties of graphs. These properties are directly useful in order to create algorithms and programs on graphs.

Before discussing these properties, we introduce some additional concepts so as to simplify the discussion that follows.

5.1 Additional concepts

We start by defining the concept of *incidence*:

Definition 5.1. *Let $G = (V, E, \phi)$ be a graph. A vertex $v \in V$ and an edge $e \in E$ are said to be* incident *if and only if $v \in \phi(e)$.*

In addition to saying that "a vertex v and an edge e are *incident*", we will also use phases such as "v is incident to e" and "e is incident to v", by which we mean the same thing.

When a graph is illustrated by a drawing, the vertex is typically drawn as a circle, and any edge incident to the vertex is drawn as a line or a curve with one end attached to the circle. When the edge is a loop, it is drawn as a curve with both ends attached to circle representing the incident vertex.

Definition 5.2. *Let* $G = (V, E, \phi)$. *A vertex* $v \in V$ *is said to be* isolated *if and only if* $\forall e \in E, v \notin \phi(e)$.

In other words, a vertex is isolated if and only if no edge is incident to it.

Another useful concept that is used in graph theory is that of *adjacency*, which can apply to two vertices or to two edges.

Two vertices are said to be *adjacent* if they share a common edge. More formally:

Definition 5.3. *Let* $G = (V, E, \phi)$ *be a graph. Two vertices* $v_1, v_2 \in V$ *are said to be* adjacent *if and only if* $\exists e \in E$ *such that* $\phi(e) = \{v_1, v_2\}$.

Notice that according to definition 5.3, a vertex v is adjacent to itself only if there is a loop that is incident to v.

Two *edges* are said to be *adjacent* if they share a common vertex. Formally:

Definition 5.4. *Let* $G = (V, E, \phi)$ *be a graph. Two edges* $e_1, e_2 \in E$ *are said to be* adjacent *if and only if* $\phi(e_1) \cap \phi(e_2) \neq \emptyset$.

5.2   Degree

The concept of *degree* is a property of vertices, and it almost corresponds to the number of edges incident to a vertex. But the presence of loops complicate things a bit, so we must be somewhat careful to get it right.

In order to be precise, we first define a different concept with the sole purpose of making the concept of degree easier to define later on. We call this concept the *contribution* of an edge to a vertex.

Definition 5.5. *Let* $G = (V, E, \phi)$ *be a graph. Let* $v \in V$ *and* $e \in E$. *The* contribution *in* G *of* e *to* v, *written* $c_G(e, v)$ *is defined as* $c_G(e, v) = 0$ *if* $v \notin \phi(e)$, $c_G(e, v) = 2$ *if* $\phi(e) = \{v\}$, *and* $c_G(e, v) = 1$ *otherwise.*

What definition 5.5 is expressing is that whenever a vertex v and an edge e are *incident* (See definition 5.1.) then e contributes some positive value to v, and if e is a loop, then that contribution is 2 units, and if it is not a loop, then it contributes 1 unit. In other words, each edge contributes 2 units *somewhere*. If the edge is a loop, then it contributes both those units to a single vertex, which is the vertex incident to the loop. If the edge is not a loop, it contributes 1 unit to each of its two incident vertices.

Definition 5.6. *Let $G = (V, E, \phi)$ be a graph. The* degree *in a graph G of a vertex $v \in V$, written $d_G(v)$ is defined as $d_G(v) = \sum_{e \in E} c_G(e, v)$.*

Before going on, let us examine in some detail what definition 5.6 means. First of all, definition 5.6 literally says that the degree of a vertex is the sum of the *contribution* of each edge of the graph to that vertex. Now, given the definition of *contribution* (See definition 5.5.), only edges *incident* to the vertex have any non-zero contribution to it. Among the edges incident to the vertex, loops each contribute 2 units to the degree, and other incident edges contribute 1 unit. Intuitively, then, the degree corresponds to the number of line segments that are drawn next to the vertex when a graph is represented as a drawing as in figure 5.1.

Thus, in the graph G in figure 5.1, $d_G(A) = 1$, $d_G(B) = 3$, $d_G(C) = 4$, $d_G(D) = 2$, $d_G(E) = 0$, $d_G(F) = 2$.

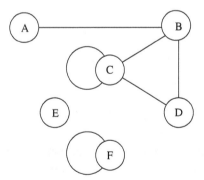

Figure 5.1: The concept of *degree*.

At this point, the reader might legitimately ask why we use the notation $c_G(e, v)$ rather than just $c(e, v)$ and $d_G(v)$ rather than just $d(v)$. The reason is that two graphs can share some vertices and some edges. Thus, it is possible that the same vertex, v have a certain degree in a graph G, and a different degree in a graph G'.

For instance, let $G = (\{A, B, C\}, \{a\}, \phi_G)$, where $\phi_G(a) = \{A, B\}$ and $G' = (\{A, B, C\}, \{a, b\}, \phi_{G'})$, where $\phi_{G'}(a) = \{A, B\}$ and $\phi_{G'}(b) = \{A, C\}$. Then we have $d_G(A) = 1$ and $d_{G'}(A) = 2$.

Figure 5.2 illustrates this situation. Clearly, figure 5.2 also shows the limitation of figures when it comes to illustrating abstract concepts like graphs. Imagine, for instance, what the graphs in figure 5.2 would look like if $\phi_{G'}(a) = \{B, C\}$ rather than $\phi_{G'}(a) = \phi_G(a) = \{A, B\}$. (See also exercise 5.3.)

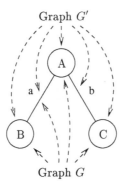

Figure 5.2: Two different degrees for the same vertex.

We are now ready to attack our first theorem. It relates the degrees of the vertices of a graph to the number of edges in that graph. Here it is:

Theorem 5.1. *Given a graph* $G = (V, E, \phi)$, $\sum_{v \in V} d_G(v) = 2|E|$.

Theorem 5.1 tells us that if we compute the degrees of each vertex of a graph G, and sum up those degrees, we obtain the same number as when we multiply the number of edges of G by 2.

Perhaps to the reader, theorem 5.1 seems obvious. Indeed, each edge contributes two units to the degree of some vertices, possibly the same if it is a loop. But the fact that it seems obvious is not enough to believe that it is true. In fact, our natural language often lets us down by a number of imprecise words and phrases. We must thus find a more formal method to make sure that it is true. That method is a *mathematical proof*, and this one will be a *proof by induction*. (See section 3.4.1.)

As it turns out, the proof of theorem 5.1 is a bit complicated, because we want to be as precise as possible. When proofs are complicated, we break them down into smaller pieces called *lemmas*. A lemma is just like a theorem, except that it may not have any particular use outside of the theorem that it was designed to simplify. Otherwise, a lemma has to be proven, just like a theorem does.

For the proof of theorem 5.1, we need a single lemma. We need it because we want to express what happens to the sum of the degrees of the vertices of a graph if we were to remove an edge from it. Intuitively, since each edge contributes 2 units, either both to a single vertex, or one unit each to two vertices, then if an edge is removed from a graph, then the sum of the degrees will drop by exactly 2. But that is "intuitively", and now we want to examine a somewhat more formal way of showing it.

To illustrate the method of the lemma, let us again take the graph G in figure 5.1, and let us consider a graph G' which is like G except that the edge between the vertices C and D is removed. Let us call that edge f. We thus have the situation illustrated by figure 5.3.

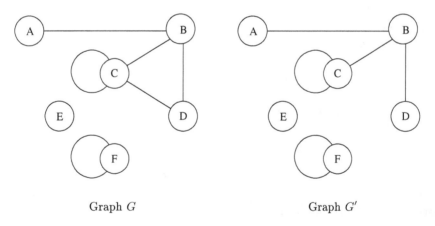

Graph G Graph G'

Figure 5.3: Illustration of lemma

What we are going to do in the lemma is to consider 4 different *views*, each one consisting of some subset of the edges and vertices of G and G'. For each view, we study the contributions of the edges of the view to the vertices of the view. Finally, we must convince ourselves that our 4 views cover the full graphs.

In the first view, illustrated by figure 5.4, we exclude f, together with its incident vertices $\phi(f)$. Clearly, as figure 5.4 illustrates, the two graphs then look the same, so they have identical contributions.

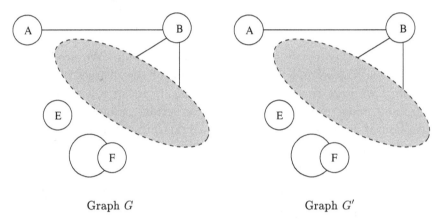

Graph G Graph G'

Figure 5.4: Illustration of lemma, view 1

In the second view, illustrated by figure 5.5, We again exclude f, but this time we keep $\phi(f)$ and exclude the other vertices. Again, the two graphs look the same, so they have identical contributions. Together, views 1 and 2 cover all vertices, and all edges except f.

In the third view, illustrated by figure 5.6, among the edges, only f is included. All the rest are excluded. Among the vertices, the ones in $\phi(f)$ are excluded. Clearly, no edge contributes to any vertex in either graph.

In the fourth and last view, illustrated by figure 5.7, again only f is included, but this time the vertices in $\phi(f)$ are included and all the others excluded. Clearly, there is a total contribution of 2 in G, and 0 in G'.

From the illustrations of figures 5.4, 5.5, 5.6, and 5.7, we conclude that the difference in total contributions is 2.

Now, let us see how that idea works a bit more formally in the lemma:

Lemma 5.1. *Let $G = (V, E, \phi)$ be a graph with $|E| > 0$. Let $f \in E$. Let*

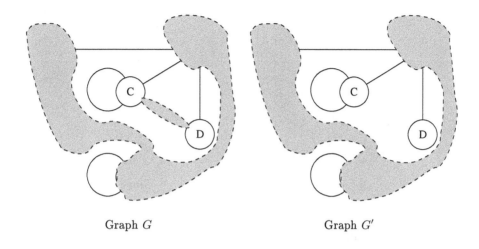

Figure 5.5: Illustration of lemma, view 2

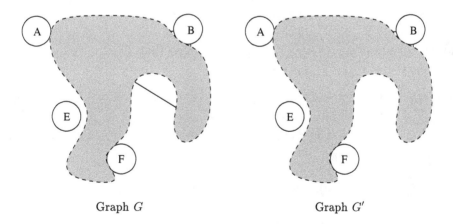

Figure 5.6: Illustration of lemma, view 3

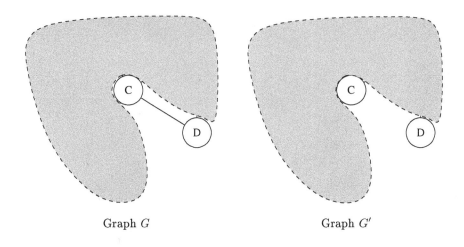

Graph G Graph G'

Figure 5.7: Illustration of lemma, view 4

$G' = (V, E \setminus \{f\}, \phi)$, *so that G' is like G with f removed. Then $\sum_{v \in V} d_G(v) = \sum_{v \in V} d_{G'}(v) + 2$.*

Proof. By the definition of degree (See definition 5.6.), for a graph $G = (E, V, \phi)$, we have that $d_G(v) = \sum_{e \in E} c_G(e, v)$ so that
$\sum_{v \in V} d_G(v) = \sum_{v \in V} \sum_{e \in E} c_G(e, v)$.
and we have that $d_{G'}(v) = \sum_{e \in E \setminus \{f\}} c_{G'}(e, v)$ so that
$\sum_{v \in V} d_{G'}(v) = \sum_{v \in V} \sum_{e \in E \setminus \{f\}} c_{G'}(e, v)$.

We break up the expression
$\sum_{v \in V} \sum_{e \in E} c_G(e, v)$ into 4 terms, so that
$\sum_{v \in V} \sum_{e \in E} c_G(e, v) = T_1 + T_2 + T_3 + T_4$ where
$T_1 = \sum_{v \in V \setminus \phi(f)} \sum_{e \in E \setminus \{f\}} c_G(e, v)$,
$T_2 = \sum_{v \in \phi(f)} \sum_{e \in E \setminus \{f\}} c_G(e, v)$,
$T_3 = \sum_{v \in V \setminus \phi(f)} c_G(f, v)$, and
$T_4 = \sum_{v \in \phi(f)} c_g(f, v)$.
Similarly, we break up the expression
$\sum_{v \in V} \sum_{e \in E} c_{G'}(e, v)$ into 2 terms, so that
$\sum_{v \in V} \sum_{e \in E} c_{G'}(e, v) = T_1' + T_2'$ where
$T_1' = \sum_{v \in V \setminus \phi(f)} \sum_{e \in E \setminus \{f\}} c_{G'}(e, v)$,
$T_2' = \sum_{v \in \phi(f)} \sum_{e \in E \setminus \{f\}} c_{G'}(e, v)$.

Now, T_1 and T_2 both exclude f so in these terms $c_G(e, v) = c_{G'}(e, v)$, and thus $T_1 = T_1'$ and $T_2 = T_2'$.

Clearly, $T_3 = 0$, because the contribution of f to any vertex other than those in $\phi(f)$ is 0.

Clearly $T_4 = 2$.

It follows that $\sum_{v \in V} d_G(v) = \sum_{v \in V} d_{G'}(v) + 2$.   □

As mentioned before, for the proof of theorem 5.1, we will use a *proof by induction*. (See section 3.4.1.) In a way, we build the graph by first adding vertices until there is the right number of vertices, but no edges. Then we add the edges one at a time until we have the graph we want. The idea is thus the following:

1. Check that $\sum_{v \in V} d_G(v) = 2|E|$ for a graph with $|E| = 0$, i.e., a graph with no edges.

2. Suppose that $\sum_{v \in V} d_G(v) = 2|E|$ for any graph with $|E| \leq k$.

3. Show that if $\sum_{v \in V} d_G(v) = 2|E|$ is true for any graph with $|E| \leq k$, it is also true for any graph with $|E| = k + 1$.

If we manage to follow this idea, we know that it is true with a graph with 0 edges, so it is true for a graph with *at most* 0 edges, so that $k = 0$. But we have proven that if it is true for a graph with at most 0 edges, it is also true for a graph with $|E| = 1$. And now that we know that it is true for a graph with $|E| = 1$, it is also true for a graph with $|E| = 2$, etc. In the end, we may conclude that it is true for a graph with any number of edges.

Now let us see how we can prove this theorem more formally:

Proof. (of theorem 5.1)

By induction on the number of edges of the graph.

1. (base case) The property is trivially true for a graph with $|E| = 0$, because the degree of every vertex in such a graph is 0.

2. (induction hypothesis) Suppose that for any graph $G = (V, E, \phi)$ with $|E| \leq k$ it holds that $\sum_{v \in V} d_G(v) = 2|E|$.

3. (induction step) Let $G = (V, E, \phi)$ be any graph such that $|E| = k{+}1$. Let $f \in E$ and consider the graph $G' = (V, E \setminus \{f\}, \phi)$, i.e. G' is like G except with one edge removed. Clearly, $|E \setminus \{f\}| = k$, so the induction hypothesis applies, and we know that $\sum_{v \in V} d_{G'}(v) = 2|E \setminus \{f\}| = 2(|E| - 1) = 2|E| - 2$. From lemma 5.1, we know that $\sum_{v \in V} d_G(v) = \sum_{v \in V} d_{G'}(v) + 2$ so that $\sum_{v \in V} d_G(v) = 2|E| - 2 + 2 = 2|E|$.

$\square$

5.3 Path

We are frequently going to need to know whether in a given graph, it is possible to go from one vertex to another vertex by following the edges. The sequence of vertices and edges we use to do that is called a *path*. In this section, we examine several possible ways of defining the concept of a path until we find the right one.

Definition 5.7. *(Caution: this definition is not good.) A* path *in a graph G is a sequence $P = v_1, v_2, \ldots, v_n$ of vertices of G such that $\forall i, 1 \le i < n$, there is an edge between v_i and v_{i+1}.*

This definition does not work very well when there are several edges between some pair of vertices. For instance, in figure 5.8, the path (according to definition 5.7), $P = A, B$ is ambiguous. We do not know whether we should use the edge a or the edge b. In some applications this ambiguity can be problematic.

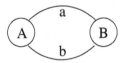

Figure 5.8: Illustration of the concept of a path.

Here is a second attempt at a definition:

Definition 5.8. *(Caution: this definition is not good.) A* path *in a graph G is a sequence $P = e_1, e_2, \ldots, e_n$ of edges of G such that $\forall i, 1 \le i < n$, e_i and e_{i+1} are adjacent.*

Unfortunately, definition 5.8 is no good either. The problem with this definition is illustrated by figure 5.9, in which a, b, c will be considered to be a path according to definition 5.8. The reason is that the edges a and b are adjacent (because of the vertex B) and edges b and c also adjacent (for the same reason). Nevertheless, we do not wish to consider a, b, c to be a path, because the idea behind a path is to start in a vertex, and then take steps, each one consisting of following an edge from the current vertex to some other vertex, ultimately ending up in a final vertex. The path a, b, c does not fulfill this criterion.

Another problem with definition 5.8 is that we do not know with which vertex the path starts.

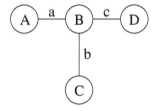

Figure 5.9: Illustration of the concept of a path.

There are several ways of repairing definitions 5.7 and 5.8. Here, we shall use the following solution:

Definition 5.9. *A path in a graph* $G = (V, E, \phi)$ *is a sequence*

$$P = v_1, e_1, v_2, e_2, \ldots, v_n, e_n, v_{n+1}$$

such that $\forall i, 1 \leq i \leq n + 1, v_i \in V$, $\forall i, 1 \leq i \leq n, e_i \in E$ *and* $\phi(e_i) = \{v_i, v_{i+1}\}$.

What definition 5.9 says is that a path is a sequence of alternating vertices and edges of the graph such that every edge is the sequence is surrounded by its incident vertices. We say that P is a path *between* v_1 *and* v_{n+1}, and sometimes that P is a path *from* v_1 *to* v_{n+1}.

With definition 5.9 we avoid the ambiguity illustrated in figure 5.8. We simply specify either the sequence A, a, B or A, b, B according to which one is wanted.

The problem with definition 5.8 also disappears with definition 5.9.

5.4   Connectivity

It is sometimes useful to be able to go from any vertex to any other vertex in the graph. For example, it would be advantageous to an airline to be able to propose to its customers that they can purchase a ticket from any airport that the airline has some flights to, to any other such airport, without having to travel with a different airline on some leg of the trip.

The concept that exactly describes this desire is called the *connectivity* of a graph. More formally:

Definition 5.10. *A graph G is* connected *if and only if $\forall v_1, v_2 \in V$, there is a path between v_1 and v_2.*

5.5   Exercises

Imagine a graph in which the vertices represent non-negative integers with exactly n binary digits (the number can start with one or more zeros), and in which there is an edge between two vertices if and only if the representation of the two binary numbers of the vertices differ in exactly one position.

For example, if $n = 2$, the vertices are 00, 01, 10, and 11, this graph has four edges: between vertices 00 and 01, between 00 and 10, between 10 and 11, and between 01 and 11.

Such a graph is called a *hypercube*.

Exercise 5.1. *Determine $|V(G)|$ as a function of n when G is a hypercube.*

Exercise 5.2. *What is the degree of the vertices of a hypercube (as a function of n)? Why?*

Exercise 5.3. *let $G = (\{A, B, C\}, \{a\}, \phi_G)$, where $\phi_G(a) = \{A, B\}$ and $G' = (\{A, B, C\}, \{a, b\}, \phi_{G'})$, where $\phi_{G'}(a) = \{B, C\}$ and $\phi_{G'}(b) = \{A, C\}$. Draw the two graphs G and G' in the same drawing so that it is clear that the two share the vertices and one of the edges. (We do not know how to do this.)*

Chapter 6

Eulerian graphs

In this chapter, we determine some necessary conditions for a graph to be "Eulerian". This word refers to the Swiss mathematician Leonhard Euler who defined and studied this concept.

6.1 Some history

In the town of Königsberg (now named Kaliningrad), there were at the time 7 bridges connecting the islands and the two river banks of the town. The configuration was the one shown in figure 6.1.

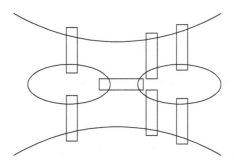

Figure 6.1: The bridges of Königsberg

The citizens of Königsberg often spent their weekends walking in the town center. Many people then asked themselves whether it was possible to start the walk on an island or on one of the banks, finish the walk on any other island or bank (or the same one) while having crossed each bridge exactly once. Nobody ever managed to find such a walk.

It is easy to see how the Königsberg problem can be modeled as a graph in which the vertices correspond to islands or banks, and in which the edges represent bridges. The problem can thus be formulated like this:

> In a graph $G = (V, E, \phi)$, is it possible to find a *path* with m edges in it, i.e., $P = v_1, e_1, v_2, e_2, \ldots, v_m, e_m, v_{m+1}$, such that $\{e_1, e_2, \ldots, e_m\} = E$ and $|E| = m$?

In other words, we must first find a path that contains every edge. In addition, the condition $|E| = m$ assures us that no edge occurs more than once in the path, because if the same edge occurs several times, but $\{e_1, e_2, \ldots, e_m\} = E$, this means that the cardinality of the set E (i.e., $|E|$) is strictly less than m.

6.2   Drawing an envelope

A problem similar to that of Königsberg (but which has a solution, contrary to that of Königsberg) concerns drawing an envelope (See figure 6.2.) without lifting the pen.

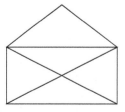

Figure 6.2: An envelope

Here, the straight-line segments correspond to the bridges of Königsberg and the intersections between the line segments correspond to islands or river banks.

Drawing an envelope is easy, provided we start drawing either in the lower-left or in the lower-right corner. If w start in any other point, it is not possible.

6.3 Formal definition

In this section, we define more formally what we mean for a graph to be "Eulerian".

Definition 6.1. *A graph $G = (V, E, \phi)$ is* Eulerian *if and only if it contains a path $P = v_1, e_1, v_2, e_2, \ldots, v_m, e_m, v_{m+1}$ such that $\{v_1, v_2, \ldots, v_m, v_{m+1}\} = V$, $\{e_1, e_2, \ldots, e_m\} = E$ and $|E| = m$.*

Let us study the consequences of definition 6.1. First of all, it means that "if we find such a path, then the graph is Eulerian", and also that "the graph is Eurlerian only if such a path can be found". In mathematics and computer science, we often use the abbreviation "iff" for "if and only if".

Second, definition 6.1 tells us that the path must have certain properties. The vertices of the path must be the set of the vertices of the graph, or in other words, the path must pass through every vertex of the graph. As an immediate consequence, a graph with an isolated vertex can not be Eulerian.

Just like the path must pass through every vertex of the graph, the path must also contain every edge of the graph. That is what the expression $\{e_1, e_2, \ldots, e_m\} = E$ means.

Finally, it must be the case that $|E| = m$, which means that the total number of edges of the graph must be the same as the number of edges of the *path*. Another way of saying that is that the path can not pass by the same edge twice. No such restriction exists for the vertices.

To summarize, definition 6.1 means "A graph is Eurlerian if and only if it contains a path that passes through each vertex at least once and that passes though each edge exactly once."

6.4   Necessary conditions for a graph to be Eulerian

In this section, we examine a certain number of *necessary conditions* in order for a graph to be Eulerian. The necessary conditions are those that are direct consequences of the fact that the graph is Eulerian. They are the properties that are true whenever the graph is Eulerian. If one of these properties is false, the graph can not be Eulerian.

6.4.1   Connectivity

The first property we examine that must necessarily be true when a graph is Eulerian is that the graph must be *connected.*.

Theorem 6.1. *If a graph G is Eulerian, then G is necessarily connected.*

Here are some other ways of stating exactly the same thing:

- Every Eulerian graph is connected.

- G Eurlerian $\Rightarrow$ G connected.

- If a graph G is not connected, then G is not Eurlerian.

- G is connected is a necessary condition for G to be Eurlerian.

How can we go about proving something like theorem 6.1? There are many possible ways. We have already seen (See section 5.2.) a proof by induction. That type of proof does not work well for this theorem. Instead, we will use a *proof by contradiction.* The idea with such a proof is to *suppose that the statement of the theorem is false*, and show that such a supposition leads to a logical contradiction. Since logic is not contradictory, it must be the supposition that is false, which shows that the statement of the theorem is true.

The first thing to do in order to prove a theorem like this is to examine the *definitions* of the concepts that it refers to. We must thus examine the definitions of "Eurlerian" and "connected". Definition 6.1 defines what it means for a graph to be Eurlerian, and definition 5.10 defines what it means for a graph to be connected.

Proof. Suppose that the statement of theorem 6.1 is false; in other words, there exists a graph G that is both Eurlerian and not connected. (It is important to realize that this phrase is the inverse of the statement of the theorem).

Now let us examine the consequences of this supposition. The graph $G = (V, E, \phi)$ is Eulerian. By the definition of Eurlerian, we know that there exists a path $P = v_1, e_1, v_2, e_2, \ldots, v_m, e_m, v_{m+1}$ such that $\{v_1, v_2, \ldots, v_m, v_{m+1}\} = V$,
$\{e_1, e_2, \ldots, e_m\} = E$ and $|E| = m$.

Now, the definition 5.10 tells us that a graph is connected if and only if $\forall v_1, v_2 \in V$, there is a path between v_1 and v_2. As we have assumed that G is *not* connected, it must be the case that $\exists w_1, w_2 \in V$, without any path between w_1 and w_2. We call them w_1 and w_2 and not v_1 and v_2 as in the definition of connectivity, in order not to mix them up with the vertices v_1 and v_2 of the definition of Eulerian.

Since P contains every vertex of G, it necessarily contains w_1 and w_2. Let us say that w_1 is the same as v_i and that w_2 is the same as v_j. We can thus write the Eulerian path like: $P = v_1, e_1, v_2, e_2, \ldots, w_1, e_i, \ldots, e_{j-1}, w_2, \ldots, v_m, e_m, v_{m+1}$. Let us examine the sub-path $P' = w_1, e_i, \ldots, e_{j-1}, w_2$ of P. A sub-path of a path is a path. P' is clearly a path between w_1 and w_2. But from the supposition, there is no path between w_1 and w_2, so we have a contradiction.

Our supposition that there exists a graph that is Eurlerian and not connected is thus false. We can conclude that every Eurlerian graph is connected. $\qquad\square$

6.4.2 Vertex parity

In this section, we investigate another necessary condition for a graph to be Eurlerian. This condition is the *parity* of the vertices of the graph. Let us start by the definition of parity:

Definition 6.2. *A vertex is said to be* even *if its degree is even. Similarly, a vertex is said to be* odd *if its degree is odd.*

The relation between the parity of the vertices of a graph and the fact that the graph is Eurlerian is expressed by the following theorem:

Theorem 6.2. *If a graph G is Eulerian, then the number of odd vertices of G is necessarily either 0 or 2.*

Before we prove theorem 6.2, let us see its consequences on the graph that represents the town of Königsberg. The degrees of the vertices of this graph are 3, 3, 3, and 5 respectively. There are 4 odd vertices. As a consequence, the graph representing the town of Königsberg is not Eulerian, which explains why the citizens of Königsberg were incapable of finding an appropriate path.

Similarly, the degrees of the vertices of the graph representing the envelope are 2, 4, 4, 4, 3, and 3. There are 2 odd vertices. The theorem does not allow us to conclude that the graph representing the envelope is Eulerian, because it is only a necessary condition, and it is important not to reverse the direction of the implication.

Let us now prove theorem 6.2. Again, it will be a proof by contradiction.

Proof. Suppose the contrary, i.e., that there exists a graph G that is Eulerian, but the number of odd vertices of G is neither 0 nor 2.

The graph $G = (V, E, \phi)$ is Eulerian. Definition 6.1 tells us that there exists a path $P = v_1, e_1, v_2, e_2, \ldots, v_m, e_m, v_{m+1}$ such that $\{v_1, v_2, \ldots, v_m, v_{m+1}\} = V$, $\{e_1, e_2, \ldots, e_m\} = E$ and $|E| = m$.

Let us look at some vertex other than v_1 and v_{m+1} in this path, and let us call it v_i. This vertex may of course occur several times in the path P. Each occurrence of v_i is surrounded by edges e_{i-1}, v_i, e_i. The two edges e_{i-1} and e_i thus contribute 2 to the degree of v_i. The degree of v_i must therefore be even.

Concerning v_1 and v_{m+1} in the path P, we distinguish two cases. The first case is when $v_1 \neq v_{m+1}$ and the second case is when $v_1 = v_{m+1}$

In the first case, the contribution of e_1 to the degree of v_1 is 1, and the contribution of e_m to the degree of v_{m+1} is also 1. The degrees of v_1 and v_{m+1} are then necessarily odd. Hence, there exist exactly 2 odd vertices in G.

In the second case, the contribution of e_1 to the degree of v_1 is 1 and the contribution of e_m to the degree of $v_{m+1} = v_1$ is also 1, for a total contribution of 2 to that vertex. That vertex is therefore even. It follows that there are no odd vertices in this case.   □

In fact, this proof helps us find the required path in a graph having 2 odd vertices (like the envelope for instance), because we can see that the path must start in one of the odd vertices and end in the other. This is why drawing the envelope, one must begin either in the lower-left corner and end in the lower-right corner in figure 6.2, or vice versa.

6.5 Sufficient conditions for a graph to be Eulerian

In the previous section, we examined two *necessary* conditions for a graph to be Eulerian. But we still do not have *sufficient* conditions for it.

Establishing sufficient conditions is considerably more difficult than establishing necessary conditions, mainly because proofs by contradiction are not well adapted to that purpose.

In fact, in order to establish sufficient conditions, a computer scientist prefers to have a *constructive* proof. Such a proof not only shows that the path required for the graph to be Eulerian *exists*, but it also suggests *a method for finding one*. The computer scientist can thus translate this method into an *algorithm* and ultimately into a *program* for finding such a path.

As it happens, the two necessary conditions already established in section 6.4 together give a sufficient condition. Without proof, here is the final theorem:

Theorem 6.3. *A graph G is Eulerian if and only if G is connected and the number of odd vertices of G is either 0 or 2.*

6.6 Exercises

Some Eulerian graphs make it easier to find the required path than others. Take a figure the shape of a rectangle, for instance. No matter where the path starts, and no matter what choice is made for a edge to exit from a vertex, in the end an acceptable path is found. Another simple example would be a tree (See definition 7.9.) that also happens to be Eulerian.

Let us call a graph *strongly Eulerian* if it is Eulerian *and* if it is always possible to find a required path in it, as suggested above.

Exercise 6.1. *Define the concept* strongly Eulerian *more formally.*

Exercise 6.2. *Find a graph with 2 odd vertices, that is not a tree, and that is strongly Eulerian.*

Exercise 6.3. *Find a graph with no odd vertices, that is not a simple cycle, and that is strongly Eulerian.*

Exercise 6.4. *Come up with some* sufficient *conditions in order for a graph to be strongly Eulerian.*

Chapter 7

Variations on graphs

In the preceding chapters, we restricted ourselves to particular kinds of graphs, namely to arbitrary undirected graphs. In this chapter, we discuss some variations on the concept of a graph that are frequently useful to different kinds of applications.

7.1   Simple graph

A *simple* graph is a graph without multiple edges; i.e., between any two vertices of the graph, there can be at most one edge.

Simple graphs are occasionally useful when only simple relations between vertices are called for. An example of such a situation would be an airline network. To determine how to go from an airport A to an airport B, it suffices to know whether the two are connected by a direct flight.

Sometimes, in order for a graph to be simple, it is also required that it has no *loops*.

7.2   Directed graph

A *directed* graph (or *digraph*) is a graph in which the edges have a direction; i.e., it is possible to distinguish the two endpoints of the edge, so that one endpoint is the *tail* of the edge and the other one is the *head* of the edge. When that is the case, the word *arc* is used rather than *edge*. When arcs are drawn in figures, the head of the arc is marked with an arrowhead.

Definition 7.1. *An* arc *is an object a with two vertex endpoints, one of which is called the* head *(written $H(a)$) and the other one is called the* tail *(written $T(a)$).*

Using definition 7.1, we can now define *directed graph*:

Definition 7.2. *A directed graph $G = (V, A)$ is a pair, where V is a set of vertices, and A is a set of arcs such that $\forall a \in A, H(a), T(a) \in V$.*

A legitimate question at this point is where the function ϕ of definition 4.1 disappeared to, and the answer is that it was replaced by the two functions H and T. Furthermore, with definition 7.1, the head and a tail are now uniquely determined by the arc itself, and are not part of the graph, as ϕ was. A direct consequence of defining it this way is that it becomes impossible in general for an arc to be in two different graphs, and the reason for doing it this way is that programs based on this definition can be faster than if an arc can occur in several different graphs with different heads and tails.

Directed graphs are often useful for modeling routes. The reason is that there might be a way to get from a point A directly to a point B, but no way to get directly from B to A. For a road network, it can be that the road is one-way, and for an airline, it might be that flights continue to other destinations without going directly back to the origin. An example of a directed graph is shown in figure 7.1.

Directed graphs are often used in computer science, because they are easier to represent in the memory of the computer than undirected graphs. In fact, undirected graphs are often represented as directed graphs in which a pair of arcs represents a single edge of an undirected graph.

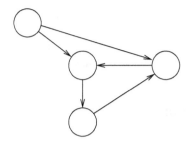

Figure 7.1: A directed graph

7.3 Acyclic graph

An interesting kind of graph is an *acyclic* graph. The main reason that acyclic graphs are interesting is that the algorithms on such graphs can be faster than in the case of a graph where cycles are permitted. When we can be sure that the graph being processed is acyclic, the programs that process it can be significantly faster. In this section, we define the concept of a cycle, and that of an acyclic graph.

Most of the graphs used in this book are undirected, so let us start with defining what a cycle is in an undirected graph.

Definition 7.3. *A cycle in an undirected graph is defined to be a* path $P = v_1, e_1, v_2, e_2, \ldots, v_n, e_n, v_{n+1}$ *such that* $v_1 = v_{n+1}$.

Now we can use definition 7.3 to define the concept of an *undirected acyclic graph*:

Definition 7.4. *An* undirected acyclic graph *is an undirected graph with no cycles.*

However, most of the graphs used in real applications are *directed*, so let us now study what it means for such a graph to be acyclic.

Let us first define the concept of a *directed path*.

Definition 7.5. *A* directed path *in a directed graph is a non-empty sequence* $P = a_1, a_2, \ldots, a_n$ *of arcs such that* $\forall i, 1 \leq i < n, H(a_i) = T(a_{i+1})$.

First of all, definition 7.5 tells us that a directed path is a sequence of arcs.

Then, it says that the sequence can not be just any sequence of arcs, but that the head of one arc in the sequence must be the tail of the next one in the sequence.

Definition 7.6. *A cycle in a directed graph is a path $P = a_1, a_2, \ldots, a_n$ such that $H(a_n) = T(a_1)$.*

This definition gives us a criterion for a path to be a cycle; i.e., that the tail of the first arc in the path must be the same as the head of the last arc in the path.

In figure 7.2, the sequence a, b, c of arcs is a cycle, as well as the sequences a, b, c, d and a, b, c, d, d, a, b, c, etc.

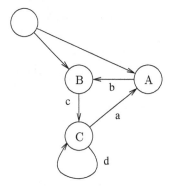

Figure 7.2: A cycle

Definition 7.7. *A cycle is* simple *if and only if a vertex can be the head of at most one arc in the cycle.*

In figure 7.2, the cycle a, b, c is simple, and so is the cycle d. In contrast, the cycle a, b, c, d is not simple, because the vertex C is the head both of the arc c and the arc d in the cycle.

In general, a directed graph can have cycles. But if that is not the case, we call it an *acyclic graph.* If it is a directed graph with no cycles, we call it a *directed acyclic graph.*

Definition 7.8. *A* directed acyclic graph *or a* DAG *is a directed graph that does not have any cycles.*

While definition 7.8 might seem trivial, it still is the first time that we have a definition of *graph without cycles*. In fundamental computer science (as well as in mathematics) we can not count on the English language to give us such definitions automatically. The fact that the English language suggests that "acyclic" means "does not have any cycles" does not give us the right to omit the definition.

Figure 7.3 shows an example of a directed acyclic graph.

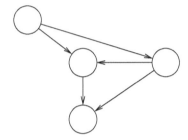

Figure 7.3: A directed acyclic graph

7.4 Tree

The concept of a *tree* is fundamental in computer science. A large number of efficient algorithms use trees. In this section, we define this concept.

First, we examine the case of undirected graphs.

Definition 7.9. *A* tree *is an undirected graph which is both* connected *and* acyclic.

In a tree, each pair of vertices is connected by a unique path, an important restriction that allows for very efficient algorithms on graphs of this kind.

Notice that definition 7.9 requires the graph to be connected. It is occasionally useful to eliminate this restriction. In that case, we frequently talk about a *forest* as being a set of mutually-disconnected trees.

Now, let us turn to the case of a directed graph.

Definition 7.10. *A directed tree is a directed acyclic graph $G = (V, A)$ in which each vertex v has an* input degree *(i.e. the number of arcs having v as a head) of 1, except for a single distinguished vertex, called the* root *of the tree, which has an input degree of 0.*

This definition tells us first of all that a directed tree is a directed acyclic graph. But there is an additional restriction, namely that the input degree of a vertex of the graph can not be greater than 1. The graph in figure 7.3 is thus not a tree because it has two vertices with an input degree of 2.

Furthermore, in a directed tree, each vertex v can be reached by a unique path from the root.

Figure 7.4 shows an example of a directed tree.

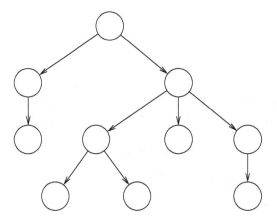

Figure 7.4: A directed tree

7.5 Exercises

A *bipartite graph* is a graph in which the vertices can be divided into two sets so that every edge in the graph goes between a vertex in one set and a vertex in the other set.

Exercise 7.1. *Provide a more formal definition of* bipartite graph. *(See the beginning of section 7.5 for an informal definition.)*

Exercise 7.2. *Determine some* sufficient conditions *in order for a graph to be bipartite. (See the beginning of section 7.5 for an informal definition of* bipartite.*) Try to make your conditions as weak as possible. For instance, a graph with no edges is trivially bipartite, but that is a very strong condition and not very useful.*

Exercise 7.3. *Prove that a tree (See definition 7.9.) is a bipartite graph. (See the beginning of section 7.5 for an informal definition of* bipartite.*)*

Part II

Algorithms

Chapter 8

The concept of an algorithm

The concept of an *algorithm* is central in computer science. In this chapter, we examine this concept in detail.

8.1   Characteristics of algorithms

The difference between an algorithm and a *program* is often only a question of *level of detail*. An algorithm is frequently expressed in a notation that is independent of any *programming language*, whereas a program is written in a particular programming language.

Another difference between an algorithm and a program is that the execution if an algorithm must always *terminate* yielding some result, whereas a program can execute in an *infinite loop* which means that it does not stop unless forced to do so by some external event (pull the power plug, for instance).

An algorithm is thus a method for solving a particular problem that is guaranteed to give an answer in finite time. The time it takes can of course be so long that it is useless for all practical purposes.

Example: In order to determine whether an integer n is a *prime number* (i.e, it contains no factors other than 1 and n), the following algorithm can be used:

For every integer i, $2 \leq i < n$, check whether i is a factor of n by dividing n by i and checking whether the result is an integer. If this is the case, halt with the answer "no". If no such value of i is a factor of n, then halt with the answer "yes".

There is a major problem with this definition of an algorithm. Let us consider that prime-number example. How can we assume that we know how to divide n by i and check that the result is an integer? Perhaps we need another algorithm for doing that as well? And if we ever find an algorithm for this division, do we not also have to find an algorithm for each step of that one? Or, on the contrary, why is it that we can not simply declare "check whether a number is prime" to be an elementary operation? If it is an elementary operation, there is no need to come up with an algorithm for it.

In other words, how do we know whether an operation is elementary, and so does not require us to come up with an algorithm for it?

The answer is that an operation is elementary when a computer can execute it *very fast*, using a relatively small number of *clock cycles*.

The reader of this book does not necessarily know whether an operation is elementary in the sense of the preceding paragraph. Luckily, that knowledge is not required either. The concept of an *abstract data type* that we examine in the following section will allow us to determine whether an operation is elementary in the sense given.

8.2   Abstract data type

Before discussing exactly what an abstract data type is, let us determine what we mean by a *data type*. Informally, a data type is a *set of objects*, usually with some obvious features in common. It is often obvious and easy to give a *name* to the type.

Example: The type named *automobile* is the set of all objects that are automobiles.

Types are not defined a priori. Any type can be defined if its definition is determined useful in some situation. Thus, a type can be arbitrarily general or arbitrarily specific according to the needs of the application. In one application, there might be no need to define the type *automobile*, but it may be useful to distinguish *organic objects* from *non-organic objects*. In another application, it might be important to distinguish automobiles with different color, so that application might have a type called *red automobile*.

However, our informal definition of the concept of a type is often not satisfactory.

For instance, the set containing the two elements "Jim" and "Jim's dog" is a type according to this definition, because it is clearly a set of objects with something in common. However, one still has a feeling that these two objects are not of the same type. Or, perhaps they are both mammals, but then the set would also contain "Anne", "the hedgehog that was just crushed by Jo's automobile", etc. It is not enough to say that the objects must "have something in common" in order for them to make up a type. We need some additional restrictions on what they have in common.

The concept of an *abstract data type* exists in order to supply this additional restriction.

Definition 8.1. *An* abstract data type *is a set of objects that admit the same* operations *so that all the operations can be applied to any object in the set.*

These operations are chosen by the computer scientist according to the requirements of the application.

Example: The operations allowed on an object of type *automobile* might be: *start, stop, fill the tank, determine the speed*, etc.

From one application to the other, the operations can be totally different, even though the name of the type might be the same. The operations possible on an object of type *person* can be quite different in an application for managing income taxes and in an application that has to do with cellular biology, for example.

8.3   The graph as an abstract data type

In this section, we discuss two ways of defining *graph* as an abstract data type. Different types generate different algorithms. Each of the data types corresponds to one of the definitions of a graph in chapter 4.

Typically, algorithms that manipulate graphs also allow modifications to the graph, such as adding or deleting a vertex or an edge. In order to simplify the algorithms, in this book, we do not allow this kind of modification.

In the first abstract data type we consider, the *edges* to play an important role. For that reason, we call this abstract data type *edge-centered*. This data type has the following operations:

1. Given a graph G, return $|V(G)|$, i.e., the number of vertices of G.

2. Given a graph G, return $|E(G)|$, i.e., the number of edges of G.

3. Given a graph G and an integer i, $0 \le i < |V(G)|$, return the vertex with that number. (Vertices are numbered from 0.)

4. Given a graph G and an integer i, $0 \le i < |E(G)|$, return the edge with that number. (Edges are numbered from 0.)

5. Given a graph G, an edge e of G, and an integer $i \in \{0,1\}$, return the first or the second vertex incident to e.

6. Given a vertex v, mark v.

7. Given a vertex v, unmark v.

8. Given a vertex v, return *true* if v is marked and *false* otherwise.

9. Given an edge e, mark e.

10. Given an edge e, unmark e.

11. Given an edge e, return *true* if e is marked and *false* otherwise.

The first four operations are necessary so that it is possible to enumerate all the vertices and all the edges of the graph. The fifth operation corresponds to the function ϕ of definition 4.1. The other operations exist so that it is possible to traverse the vertices and the edges of the graph and to determine whether a particular vertex or a particular edge has already been traversed.

The operations of the edge-centered abstract data types are formalized in the following way. Each operation includes its *name* and its *parameters*:

1: `VERTEX_COUNT(G)`
2: `EDGE_COUNT(G)`
3: `VERTEX(G, i)`
4: `EDGE(G, i)`
5: `EDGE_END(G, e, i)`

6: `MARK_VERTEX(s)`
7: `UNMARK_VERTEX(s)`
8: `VERTEX_MARKED(s)`
9: `MARK_EDGE(e)`
10: `UNMARK_EDGE(e)`
11: `EDGE_MARKED(e)`

The second abstract data type we consider is similar to the first, but this time the *vertices* play a more important role than the edges. For that reason, we call this abstract data type *vertex centered*. This data type has the following operations:

1. Given a graph G, return $|V(G)|$, i.e., the number of vertices of G.

2. Given a graph G and an integer i, $0 \leq i < |V(G)|$, return the vertex with that number. (Vertices are numbered from 0.)

3. Given a graph G, a vertex v of G, return the number of edges incident to v in G.

4. Given a graph G, a vertex v of G, and an integer i, return the ith edge incident to v.

5. Given a graph G, a vertex v, and an edge e incident to v, return the other vertex incident to e.

6. Given a vertex v, mark v.

7. Given a vertex v, unmark v.

8. Given a vertex v, return *true* if v is marked and *false* otherwise.

9. Given an edge e, mark e.

10. Given an edge e, unmark e.

11. Given an edge e, return *true* if e is marked and *false* otherwise.

Here, the third and fourth operations correspond to the function ψ of definition 4.2. The fifth operation is (strictly speaking) not needed, but it is included because it makes the algorithms faster, and it can be considered a primitive operation.

The operations of the vertex-centered abstract data types are formalized in the following way. As before, each operation includes its *name* and its *parameters*:

```
1: VERTEX_COUNT(G)          6:  MARK_VERTEX(s)
2: VERTEX(G, i)             7:  UNMARK_VERTEX(s)
3: EDGE_COUNT(G, v)         8:  VERTEX_MARKED(s)
4: EDGE(G, v, i)            9:  MARK_EDGE(e)
5: FOLLOW_EDGE(G, v, e)    10:  UNMARK_EDGE(e)
                           11:  EDGE_MARKED(e)
```

8.4 Asymptotic complexity

In this section, we discuss a very important characteristic of an algorithm, namely its *performance*. Even though the speed of computers steadily increases, it will never be sufficient, simply because users will want to solve more and more complex problems. Besides, for a large number of algorithms, doubling the speed of the computer does not mean that we can solve a problem twice the size.

It is therefore imperative for the computer scientist to choose the algorithm that is the fastest for the job. However, there is a problem with this requirement, namely that the execution speed of an algorithm depends on the computer (the kind of processor, kind and amount of memory, sometimes the kind of disk). How, then, can we compare algorithms with respect to performance if we do not necessarily know on what computer the algorithm will ultimately run?

In addition to depending on the computer, the execution time of an algorithm, of course, depends on the size of the problem to solve. In order to compare the performance of two algorithms, we would have to give the size of the problem as well, and the result of the comparison may depend on the size of the problem.

These questions are studied by a branch of computer science known as *complexity theory*. Here, we are particularly interested in the concept of *asymptotic complexity*.

The basic idea is to not measure the execution time directly, but to *count the number of elementary operations* (additions, subtractions, comparisons, etc.) required for its execution *as a function of the size of the problem*. We call this function the *time function* of the algorithm. Unfortunately, the time function does not allow us to determine precisely the execution time of an algorithm, and thus to compare two algorithms precisely with respect to execution time. The reason is that an elementary operation can take more or less time to execute according to the computer on which it runs.

In order to get around this problem, computer scientists developed *asymptotic complexity*. Using asymptotic complexity, we do not give the exact execution time of an algorithm, but only an approximation of it. This approximation is formulated as a well-known function that gives the *general form* of the time function.

Example: Let us take an algorithm with an execution time that on a particular computer is $t(n) = 21n^3$, where n is the *size* of the problem. If it is a graph problem, n might, for instance, then be the number of vertices of the graph. The corresponding asymptotic complexity will then be n^3; i.e., we ignore the constant factor 21 and only look at the *general form* of the function. This approximation allows us to forget the difference between different computers, because on a different computer, the execution time of this algorithm might be $t(n) = 5n^3$ or $t(n) = 56n^3$, but computers are sufficiently similar that the general form of the function will not change. Thus, independently of the computer, the asymptotic complexity of the algorithm is n^3. Again, unfortunately, the approximations introduced by asymptotic complexity do not allow us to compare two algorithms with time functions that have the same general form, but that comparison would be difficult *anyway*, given the difference in execution time of elementary operations between different computers. On the positive side, as we shall see later in this section, comparing two different algorithms with time functions with *different* general forms becomes possible, and it becomes meaningful to do so without taking into account the difference in execution time of elementary operations between different computers.

The notation used to indicate that an approximation of the real time function is given is called *big-O notation* simply because it uses the capital letter 'O'. Thus, we say that an algorithm with $t(n) = 21n^3$ has an asymptotic complexity (or just *complexity*) of $O(n^3)$ (pronounced "big Oh of n cubed", "Oh of n cubed", or "Oh of n to the three").

Because of the way the asymptotic complexity is computed, it does not allow us to distinguish between two different algorithms with time functions that have the same general form but different constant factors. However, this is on purpose, because such a comparison is not necessarily useful, given that one algorithm can run faster on one computer, and the other algorithm can run faster on another computer. The important aspect of asymptotic complexity, though, is that it allows us to compare different algorithms where the time function has a *different general form*.

Example: To sort a table of n numbers in increasing order, there exists an algorithm called *insertion sort* with an asymptotic complexity of $O(n^2)$. There is another one called *heap sort* with a complexity of $O(n \log n)$. Which one is faster? In general $O(n^2) > O(n \log n)$ which tells us that *heap sort* is faster than *insertion sort*. While it is *possible* that for insertion sort $t(n) = 2n^2$ and that for *heap sort* $t(n) = 1000n \log_2 n$, so that for many values of n the latter takes longer; fortunately, this situation almost never occurs. It is thus reasonable to conclude that heap sort is faster than insertion sort. This is especially true when n becomes large, and that is also when we are the most interested in choosing an efficient algorithm. In that example, $2n^2$ is greater than $1000n \log_2 n$ starting at values of n of a little more than 6000. In other words, if the table to sort has more than around 6000 elements (which is a modest size, so this is often the case), then the algorithm with a complexity of $O(n \log n)$ is faster than the one with a complexity of $O(n^2)$ even if the constant is 500 times bigger. But again, this situation almost never occurs, so in reality, an algorithm with a complexity of $O(n \log n)$ is usually faster than an algorithm with a complexity of $O(n^2)$ even when n is relatively small, say around 10 or 20.

An important goal of the study of algorithms is to find algorithms that are efficient as far as asymptotic complexity is concerned. In addition, it is sometimes possible to prove that the algorithm thus found is *optimal* in that no other algorithm can possibly have a better asymptotic complexity. In the case of sorting for instance, we can prove that if we are only allowed to use comparisons to determine which number is larger, then no algorithm can have an asymptotic complexity less than $O(n \log n)$. Such a result is of great importance, because it allow us to avoid wasting time and effort trying to find a better algorithm where no such algorithm can possibly exist.

8.5 Exercises

Exercise 8.1. *Imagine you need to sort a deck of cards. Initially, the unsorted deck of cards is in one stack, face down. You can use at most two additional stacks, and you can only look at the top-card of each stack. After having looked at any two top cards, you can decide to move one or the other to the top of another stack. Invent an algorithm that, when it terminates, leaves all the cards sorted in one stack. What is the complexity of your algorithm?*

Exercise 8.2. *Imagine you are in a maze of rooms, all connected to each other by tunnels. Every room is identical except for the number of doors it has. Each door leads to a long confusing tunnel, which at the end winds up in another room. Your task is to count the number of rooms. You have at your disposal an infinite supply of beads with identical color and shape. You can leave a bead behind in a room or in a tunnel, and you can pick up a bead that you previously left. Invent an algorithm for this task. Can you estimate its complexity?*

Chapter 9

Graph algorithms

In this chapter, we study a certain number of algorithms on graphs. We will use both abstract data types discussed in chapter 8, and we will analyze their influence on the asymptotic complexity of the algorithms that result.

9.1 Degree of a vertex

The first algorithm we present is a simple algorithm for computing the *degree* of a vertex (See definition 5.6.) Computing the degree of a vertex is relatively easy in the case of the vertex-centered abstract data type, and somewhat harder in the case of the edge-centered abstract data type. We start with the algorithm for the edge-centered abstract data type, which is shown in algorithm 9.1.

Algorithm 9.1.
Input: A graph G using the edge-centered abstract data type and a vertex v.
Output: The degree of v in G.
Algorithm:

1. *Initialize an accumulator to 0.*

2. *Use the operation EDGE_COUNT(G) to obtain $|E(G)|$, and store the result in the variable named ec.*

3. *For i from* 0 *to ec* − 1 *do*

    (a) *Use the operation* EDGE(G, i) *to obtain the ith edge of G, and store the result in the variable named e.*

    (b) *Use the operation* EDGE_END(G, e, 1) *to obtain the first vertex incident to e in G, and store the result in the variable named w.*

    (c) *If v = w then increment the accumulator.*

    (d) *Use the operation* EDGE_END(G, e, 2) *to obtain the second vertex incident to e in G, and store the result in the variable named w.*

    (e) *If v = w then increment the accumulator.*

4. *Return the value of the accumulator.*

In algorithm 9.1 we use the concept of an *accumulator* which is just a *local variable* that holds some measure to be counted during the course of the execution of the algorithm. Here, the accumulator contains the *contribution* (See definition 5.5.) to the degree of the vertex of the edges processed so far. Typically, the accumulator is initialized to contain 0, as is the case of algorithm 9.1.

After initializing the accumulator, algorithm 9.1 executes a *loop*[1] for each edge of the graph. In the body of the loop, the two vertices incident to the edge are examined, and if either of them is the vertex passed as an argument, then we *increment* (i.e., add 1 to) the accumulator. If the edge is a loop so that both endpoints are the same vertex, and that vertex happens to be the one passed as an argument, then the accumulator is incremented twice in this iteration of the loop.

Finally, algorithm 9.1 returns the contents of the accumulator.

Clearly, the body of the loop of algorithm 9.1 is executed as many times as there are edges in the graph. This is not good news, because if the graph is big, while the degree of each individual vertex is small, then algorithm 9.1 will still take considerable time to compute the degree of a single vertex.

When we use the vertex-centered abstract data type, computing the degree of

---

[1]There are two concepts of a *loop* in this book. One is that a loop is an edge incident to a single vertex, and the other is an instruction in a program or in an algorithm that allows repetition of other instructions.

a vertex is easier, not in the sense that the algorithm is shorter, but in that it is more efficient. Algorithm 9.2 shows the method.

Algorithm 9.2.
Input: A graph G using the edge-centered abstract data type and a vertex v.
Output: The degree of v in G.
Algorithm:

1. *Initialize an accumulator to 0.*

2. *Use the operation* **EDGE_COUNT** *(G, v) to obtain the number of edges incident to v in G, and store the result in the variable named ec.*

3. *For i from 0 to ec − 1 do*

   (a) *Increment the accumulator.*
   (b) *Use the operation* **EDGE** *(G, v, i) to obtain the ith edge incident to v in G, and store the result in the variable named e.*
   (c) *Use the operation* **FOLLOW_EDGE** *(G, v, e) to obtain the other vertex incident to e in G, and store the result in the variable named w.*
   (d) *If v = w then increment the accumulator.*

4. *Return the value of the accumulator.*

Contrary to algorithm 9.1, algorithm 9.2 does not examine each edge of the graph, and, in fact, the vertex-centered abstract data type used here does not make it easy to do so. Instead, it just examines the edges incident to the vertex for which we want to compute the degree.

Again, algorithm 9.2 starts by initializing an accumulator. It then executes a loop for each edge incident to the vertex. Clearly, any edge incident to the vertex must contribute some non-zero amount to the degree of the vertex (See definition 5.5.), so algorithm 9.2 can safely increment the accumulator for each iteration of the loop. However, it is possible that the edge contributes a value of 2 to the degree of this vertex, and that is the case if this edge is a loop. Algorithm 9.2 detects this case, by examining the opposite endpoint of the edge. If the opposite endpoint is also this vertex, then the accumulator is incremented a second time.

Finally, algorithm 9.2 returns the value of the accumulator.

From the point of view of asymptotic complexity, algorithm 9.2 is much more efficient than algorithm 9.1. The reason for this is all in the difference in abstract data types. The edge-centered abstract data type allows easy access to all the edges of the graph, but makes it hard to determine which edges are incident to a particular vertex (something we need in order to compute the degree), whereas the vertex-centered abstract data type has operations to access exactly the edges incident to a particular vertex. So for *this particular problem*, the vertex-centered abstract data type gives a more efficient algorithm. For other algorithms, the edge-centered abstract data type yields a more efficient algorithm

To be precise about the complexity of algorithm 9.2, it is $O(d)$ where d is the degree of the vertex. In the worst case, all the edges of the graph are incident to the vertex for which we want to compute the degree, so in the worst case, the algorithm still has a complexity of $O(|E(G)|)$.

It would be fairly easy to include a primitive operation in both abstract data types to give the degree of a vertex immediately. The degree would simply be stored together with each vertex, a change which would give a complexity of $O(1)$ for this operation.

9.2   Average degree

According to definition 5.6, the *degree* of a vertex is equal to the sum of the *contributions* (See definition 5.5.) of each edge of the graph to the vertex. For the purpose of this section, we define *average degree* of a graph like this:

Definition 9.1. *The* average degree *of a graph G, written $\overline{d}(G)$ is defined by:*

$$\overline{d}(G) = \frac{\sum_{v \in V(G)} d_G(v)}{|V(G)|}$$

The purpose of this section is to find different algorithms for computing the average degree of a graph.

For the *edge-centered* abstract data type, the work is almost trivial. We simply apply theorem 5.1 that gives us $\sum_{v \in V(G)} d_G(v)$ as a function of $|E(G)|$, and then we divide this quantity by $|V(G)|$.

Here is description of the algorithm in a more conventional algorithmic form:

Algorithm 9.3. *Input: A graph G using the edge-centered abstract data type. Output: The average degree of G. Algorithm:*

1. *Use the operation* `VERTEX_COUNT(G)` *to obtain* $|V(G)|$, *and store the result in the variable named vc.*

2. *Use the operation* `EDGE_COUNT(G)` *to obtain* $|E(G)|$, *and store the result in the variable named ec.*

3. *Multiply ec by 2 in order to obtain the sum of the degrees as theorem 5.1 stipulates, and store the result in the variable named ec.*

4. *Divide ec by vc and return the result.*

This algorithm is particularly simple. It contains neither tests nor loops. In fact, its execution time is constant, independent of the size (here, the number of edges) of the graph. In that case, we say that the asymptotic complexity of the algorithm is $O(1)$. This means that the general form of the time function of this algorithm is the same as that of the constant function $f(n) = 1$, i.e., a function that for every value of n returns 1. An algorithm of this complexity is optimal. We have thus found the best algorithm for computing the average degree of a graph. Unfortunately, this algorithm is only possible when the edge-centered abstract data type is available.

If instead we use the vertex-centered abstract data type, we must examine each vertex in order to determine the sum of the degrees. Here is one possible algorithm:

Algorithm 9.4. *Input: A graph G using the vertex-centered abstract data type. Output: The average degree of G. Algorithm:*

1. *Initialize an accumulator to 0.*

2. *Use the operation* `VERTEX_COUNT(G)` *to obtain* $|V(G)|$, *and store the result in the variable named vc.*

3. *For i from* 0 *to* $vc - 1$ *do*

    (a) *Use the operation* `VERTEX(G, i)` *to obtain the* i^{th} *vertex of G, and store the result in the variable named v.*

    (b) *Use algorithm 9.2 to obtain the degree of v, and store the result in the variable named deg.*

    (c) *Add the contents of the variable deg to the accumulator.*

4. *Divide the accumulator by vc and return the result.*

The complexity of algorithm 9.4 is a bit tricky to establish, because it is easy to over-estimate it. Clearly, algorithm 9.4 contains a loop with $|V(G)|$ iterations. In each iteration, a call to algorithm 9.2 is made, and, as explained in section 9.1, the worst case complexity of computing the degree of a vertex using the vertex-centered abstract data type is $O(|E(G)|)$. The combination of these two values might suggest that the complexity of algorithm 9.4 is $O(|V(G)| \cdot |E(G)|)$, but that value can never be obtained for any graph, because it would be required that every edge of the graph is incident to every vertex, which clearly can not be the case, other than for very small graphs. A more optimistic (and more accurate) estimate of the complexity of algorithm 9.4 is $O(|E(G)| + |V(G)|$. As explained in section 9.1, the complexity of algorithm 9.2 is really $O(d)$ where d is the degree of the vertex for which the degree is computed. Since algorithm 9.4 calls algorithm 9.2 for each vertex, the total number of iterations can only be $O(|E(G)|$ (See also theorem 5.1.), except that we must compensate for vertices with a degree of 0 (it does not take 0 time to determine that the degree of a vertex is 0), so in order to obtain the complexity of algorithm 9.4, we must also allow some time for each vertex, in case there are many vertices with no incident edges. The best estimate for the complexity of algorithm 9.4 is thus $O(|E(G)| + |V(G)|)$.

9.3   Connectivity

In this section, we study another algorithmic problem, namely that of *connectivity*. We would like an algorithm that, given an arbitrary graph G, answers "yes" if and only if G is *connected* and "no" if it is not.

A simple idea would be to use definition 5.10 directly, and verify whether between every pair of vertices v_1 and v_2 there exists a path. Let us study this idea a bit more closely.

The algorithm would then be (for both abstract data types):

Algorithm 9.5.
Input: A graph G.
Output: A Boolean value indicating whether G is connected or not.
Algorithm:

1. *Use the operation* **VERTEX_COUNT** *(G) to obtain* $|V(G)|$, *and store the result in the variable named vc.*

2. *For i from 0 to vc − 1 do*

    (a) *Use the operation* **VERTEX** *(G, i) to obtain the* i^{th} *vertex of G, and store the result in the variable named v.*

    (b) *For j from 0 to vc − 1 do*

        i. *Use the operation* **VERTEX** *(G, j) to obtain the* j^{th} *vertex of G, and store the result in the variable named w.*

        ii. *Check whether there is a path between v and w.*

        iii. *If not, return the value false, because G is not connected.*

3. *Return true, because if we come here without having returned false, then there must exist a path between every pair of vertices.*

Notice that this algorithm uses a non-elementary operation, namely "Check whether there is a path between v and w". This is not a problem per se, except that:

1. We must come up with an algorithm for this operation.

2. We must be careful when we determine the complexity of algorithm 9.5, because we have to take into account the complexity of the sub-algorithm that it calls.

So, let us now see how we can solve the problem of finding a path between any pair of vertices v and w. The algorithm for doing that will depend on the abstract data type that we choose.

But before we look at possible solutions, we need another definition:

Definition 9.2. *A path $P = v_1, e_1, v_2, e_2, \ldots, v_n, e_n, v_{n+1}$ is said to be* simple *if and only if $\forall i, j \in [1, n]$, $v_i = v_j \Rightarrow i = j$ and $\forall i, j \in [2, n+1]$, $v_i = v_j \Rightarrow i = j$.*

Definition 9.2 tells us that if two vertices at place i and j in the path are the same, then i and j are also the same. In other words, "a vertex can not occur more than once in the path". So in order for a path to be simple, it can not pass through the same vertex twice. However, definition 9.2 allows for the *first* and the *last* vertices to be the same, and in that case, the path is a *cycle*.

We use definition 9.2 in order to come up with a theorem that will help us find a path between two vertices of a graph.

Theorem 9.1. *In a graph G, if there exists a path between the vertex $v \in V(G)$ and the vertex $w \in V(G)$, then there exists a simple path between v and w.*

Proof. Let $P = v_1, e_1, v_2, e_2, \ldots, v_n, e_n, v_{n+1}$ be the path between the two vertices $v = v_1$ and $w = v_{n+1}$. If P is already simple, then there trivially exists a simple path between v and w. If not (i.e., if P is not simple), then, according to definition 9.2, there are either two vertices v_i and v_j such that $i, j \in [1, n]$, for which $i \neq j$ but $v_i = v_j$ or else two vertices v_i and v_j such that $i, j \in [2, n + 1]$, for which $i \neq j$ and $v_i = v_j$. Assuming $i < j$ (if not we swap the roles of the two), we can write P in the following way: $P = v_1, e_1, \ldots, v_i, e_i, \ldots, v_j, e_j, \ldots, v_n, e_n, v_{n+1}$.

From P we can then construct a shorter path P' in which the number of occurrences of vertices $v_i = v_j$ is fewer than the number of occurrences of vertices $v_i = v_j$ in P, by removing from P the part $e_i, \ldots, v_j$. We obtain $P' = v_1, e_1, \ldots, v_i, e_j, \ldots, v_n, e_n, v_{n+1}$.

That P' is shorter than P is obvious. That the number of occurrences of v_i has decreased is also obvious. But how can we be sure that P' is a path? In order to do that, we must again look at definition 5.9. In this definition, it is required that each edge of the path must be surrounded by its incident vertices. In P', this requirement is obviously fulfilled for all edges except e_j which no longer has v_j on its left. Luckily, $v_i = v_j$, an observation which solves the problem.

Now, we only have to repeat the method of shortening the path until it is simple. □

This proof is special, because not only does it tell us that there exists a simple path, but it also tells us *how to construct it* from a path that is not simple. Such a proof, i.e., a proof that not only tells us that some object exists, but also gives us a method for finding it, is called a *constructive proof*. Such a proof is always more appreciated by computer scientists than a proof that only indicates that an object exists. The reason for this preference is that a computer scientist can often convert a constructive proof into an algorithm for finding the object (though we will not use this possibility in this particular case). Furthermore, a constructive proof is always more convincing than a proof of existence only.

We use theorem 9.1 in order to come up with an algorithm that finds a *simple path* instead of some arbitrary path. An algorithm for finding a simple path is not only faster than an algorithm for finding an arbitrary path, but it is also easier to write and easier to understand.

Theorem 9.2. *In a graph G, there exists a simple path between two vertices v and w if and only if either $v = w$ or there exists a simple path between vertex v' adjacent to v (See definition 5.3.) such that the path between v' and w does not contain v.*

Proof. This theorem is a bit hard to prove. First of all, the statement of theorem 9.2 contains the phrase "if and only if", so that we must prove both "if" and "only if". Usually, they are proven separately.

("if" part): We must prove that IF either $v = w$ or there exists a simple path between v' and w (where v' is adjacent to v) that does not contain v, THEN there is a simple path between v and w. If $v = w$, then there trivially exists a simple path between v and w, namely the path $P = v$. If there exists a simple path between a vertex v' adjacent to v and w which does not contain v, then we can write this path as follows: $P = v', \ldots, w$. Let e be some edge (there might be more than one) incident to both v and v'. By the definitions of adjacency (See definition 5.3.) and incidence (See definition 5.1.) we know that such an edge exists. From P, v and e, we can construct $P' = v, e, v', \ldots, w$.

It is clear that P' is a path because the restrictions of incidence are respected. Furthermore, P' is simple because P is simple and v does not occur in P. We conclude that P' is a simple path between v and w, which concludes this part of the proof.

("only if" part): We must prove that if there exists a simple path between two vertices v and w, then either $v = w$ or there exists a simple path between some vertex v' adjacent to v and w that does not contain v. In order to do that, we examine the length of the path P that exists between v and w. If P contains a single vertex (i.e. $P = v$), then by definition of path (See definition 5.9.) $v = w$. Otherwise, (if P contains more than one vertex), we can write it $P = v, e, v', \ldots, w$ (possibly with $v' = w$). Now, $P' = v', \ldots, w$ is a simple path between v' and w. By definitions 5.9 and 5.3, v and v' are necessarily adjacent, which concludes this part of the proof.   □

Now we can start thinking about an algorithm for finding a simple path between two vertices v and w. Here is an attempt:

Algorithm 9.6.
Input: A graph G and two vertices $v, w \in V(G)$.
Output: A Boolean value indicating whether there is a simple path containing only initially unmarked vertices between v and w in G.
Side effects: Some vertices might be marked as a result of executing this algorithm.
Algorithm:

1. *If $v = w$, then return with a value of true.*

2. *Use the operation* MARK_VERTEX(v) *to mark the vertex v.*

3. *For every vertex v' adjacent to v do:*

    (a) *Use the operation* VERTEX_MARKED(v') *to check whether the vertex v' is marked.*

    (b) *If it is not marked:*

        i. *Check whether there is a simple path between v' and w.*

        ii. *If such is the case, then return true.*

> *4. We come here if no simple path has been found between any vertex v' adjacent to v and w. Return false.*

Algorithm 9.6 is much more complicated than the ones we have studied so far. For one thing, it is *recursive*; i.e., in the algorithm that is meant to check whether there exists a path, we use the same algorithm to verify that there exists a path. With recursive algorithms, we must make sure that it always *terminates*. (Otherwise, according to section 8.1, it is not an algorithm.) However, we will not attempt to prove termination here.

Another complicating factor is that the algorithm as described does *not* always do what we set out to do, namely return *true* if and only if there is a simple path between v and w. Instead, it returns *true* if and only if there is a simple path between v and w *containing only initially unmarked vertices*. The two are the same only if before the first call, we make sure that all the vertices of the graph are unmarked, so we must remember to do that before attempting to use algorithm 9.6. The reason for designing an algorithm that does not do exactly what we initially want, is that by changing the design slightly, we can make use of the same algorithm in the recursive call.

In algorithm 9.6 we have hidden a slight complicating factor. The algorithm says "For every vertex v' adjacent to v do", but this is not so simple to do. With the edge-centered abstract data type, we do not have direct access to the adjacent vertices. For this abstract data type, we must thus write something like this:

Algorithm 9.7.
Input: A graph G and two vertices $v, w \in V(G)$.
Output: A Boolean value indicating whether there is a simple path containing only initially unmarked vertices between v and w in G.
Side effects: Some vertices might be marked as a result of executing this algorithm.
Algorithm:

> *1. If $v = w$ then return with a value of true.*
>
> *2. Use the operation MARK_VERTEX(v) to mark the vertex v.*
>
> *3. Use the operation EDGE_COUNT(G) to obtain $|E(G)|$, and store the result in the variable named ec.*

4. *For i from 0 to ec − 1 do*

   (a) *Use the operation **EDGE**(G, i) to obtain the ith edge of G, and store the result in the variable named e.*

   (b) *Use the operation **EDGE_END**(G, e, 1) to obtain the first vertex incident to e in G, and store the result in the variable named a.*

   (c) *Use the operation **EDGE_END**(G, e, 2) to obtain the second vertex incident to e in G, and store the result in the variable named b.*

   (d) *store nil in v′.*

   (e) *If a = v and b ≠ v then store b in v′.*

   (f) *If b = v and a ≠ v then store a in v′.*

   (g) *If v′ ≠ nil then*

       i. *Use the operation **VERTEX_MARKED**(v′) to check whether the vertex v′ is marked.*

       ii. *If it is not marked, then*

           A. *Check whether there is a simple path between v′ and w.*

           B. *If such is the case, then return true.*

5. *We come here if no simple path has been found between any vertex v′ adjacent to v and w. Return false.*

If we use the vertex-centered abstract data type, the algorithm is faster and simpler:

Algorithm 9.8.
Input: A graph G and two vertices v, w ∈ V(G).
Output: A Boolean value indicating whether there is a simple path containing only initially unmarked vertices between v and w in G.
Side effects: Some vertices might be marked as a result of executing this algorithm.
Algorithm:

1. *If v = w then return with a value of true.*

2. *Use the operation **MARK_VERTEX**(v) to mark the vertex v.*

3. *Use the operation* `EDGE_COUNT(G, v)` *to obtain the number of edges incident to v in G, and store the result in the variable named ec.*

4. *For i from 0 to ec − 1 do*

    (a) *Use the operation* `EDGE(G, v, i)` *to obtain the ith edge incident to v in G, and store the result in the variable named e.*

    (b) *Use the operation* `FOLLOW_EDGE(G, v, e)` *to obtain the other vertex incident to e in G, and store the result in the variable named v'.*

    (c) *Use the operation* `VERTEX_MARKED(v')` *to check whether the vertex v' is marked.*

    (d) *If it is not marked:*

        i. *Check whether there is a simple path between v' and w.*

        ii. *If such is the case, then return true.*

5. *We come here if no simple path has been found between any vertex v' adjacent to v and w. Return false.*

With respect to the asymptotic complexity of these algorithms, let us have a look at the case of the edge-centered abstract data type (algorithm 9.7). The execution time depends on the number of vertices in the simple path between v and w. While it is possible that such paths might be short, the algorithm still iterates for each edge in the graph. Thus, the execution time is then at least proportional to the number of edges of the graph, or using big-O notation, the execution time is $O(|E(G)|)$. In general, however, it is even greater because of the number of vertices as well.

Now let us consider algorithm 9.5 for checking whether a graph is connected. It has two nested loops, each loop being executed for each vertex of the graph. Each time the body of the inner loop is executed, we call algorithm 9.7 or algorithm 9.8 in order to find a simple path. The complexity of this algorithm is thus at least $O(|V(G)|^2|E(G)|)$. In other words, the execution time is proportional to the square of the number of vertices multiplied by the number of edges. This is not so good. A telecommunications company, for instance, can easily have a million customers (vertices) and a million possibilities for a call to be made (edges). That situation would give 10^{18} operations to execute. Even if we assume that the computer is able to execute one elementary operation per clock cycle (which is unlikely), and the computer can execute 10^9 cycles per second (definitely possible), checking such a graph to verify that every customer can call every other customer would require 10^9 seconds of computer time for the company. Given that a year has around $3 \cdot 10^7$ seconds, this verification would take roughly 30 years of computation. The real value is almost certainly much higher.

It is thus out of the question to suggest such an algorithm for a telecommunications company. But what can we do?

The answer is again in a theoretical result about graphs. In fact, the performance problem described above is due to the fact that we apply definition 5.10 directly. We now show a result that allows us to do much better.

Theorem 9.3. *A graph G is connected if and only if from any vertex $v \in V(G)$, there is a path to every other vertex of G.*

Proof. ("if" part): We must prove that if from any vertex $v \in V(G)$ there exists a path between v and every other vertex of G, then G is connected. Recall that the definition of connectivity (See definition 5.10.) requires that $\forall v_1, v_2 \in V(G)$, there is a path between v_1 and v_2. The question thus becomes: Is it the case that if from any vertex $v \in V(G)$ there exists a path to every other vertex of G, then $\forall v_1, v_2 \in V(G)$, there is a path between v_1 and v_2?

For this part, we use the technique of proof by contradiction; i.e, we suppose that from any vertex $v \in V(G)$, there is a path to every other vertex of the graph, but $\exists v_1, v_2 \in V(G)$ with no path between v_1 and v_2, and then we show that this assumption leads to a contradiction.

Our assumption says that there exists a pair v_1 and v_2 with no path between them. The advantage of a proof by contradiction is that we only have to examine one such pair of vertices. We known that there exists a path between v and every other vertex, in particular there exists a path between v and v_1 and a path between v and v_2. Let us call those paths $P_1 = v, \ldots, v_1$ and $P_2 = v, \ldots, v_2$. We first look at the reverse path of P_1, that is $\overline{P_1} = v_1, \ldots, v$. Now $\overline{P_1}$ is clearly a path between v_1 and v. Next, we look at the concatenation of $\overline{P_1}$ and P_2, i.e., $\overline{P_1}P_2 = v_1, \ldots, v, \ldots, v_2$. $\overline{P_1}P_2$ is a path between v_1 and v_2 which contradicts the assumption that no such path exists, which proves the "if" part of the proof.

("only if" part): We must prove that if a graph is connected, then from any vertex $v \in V(G)$, there exists a path to every other vertex of the graph. This part is trivial, because according to definition 5.10, there is such a path from every vertex of the graph to every other vertex of the graph, and thus in particular from v to every other vertex.

Both the "if" and the "only if" part now being proved, the proof is finished. □

With the result of theorem 9.3, we can improve algorithm 9.5 as follows:

Algorithm 9.9.
Input: A graph G.
Output: A Boolean value indicating whether G is connected or not.
Algorithm:

1. *Use the operation* **VERTEX**(G, 0) *to obtain the 0th vertex of G, and store the result in the variable named v.*

2. *Use the operation* **VERTEX_COUNT**(G) *to obtain $|V(G)|$, and store the result in the variable named vc.*

3. *For i from 0 to $vc - 1$ do*

    (a) *Use the operation* **VERTEX**(G, i) *to obtain the ith vertex of G, and store the result in the variable named w.*

    (b) *Check whether there is a path between v and w.*

    (c) *If that is not the case, return with a value of $false$.*

4. *Return with a value of $true$, because if we come here, there exists a path from v to every other vertex.*

The nested loop of algorithm 9.5 has been replaced by a single operation to access vertex number 0 of G. For a graph with 10^6 vertices, we have thus improved the execution time by a factor 10^6. If for a given problem, algorithm 9.5 has an execution time of 30 years (around 10^9 seconds), then the execution time of algorithm 9.9 can be expected to be around 10^3 second, or around 17 minutes.

The improvement in execution time is impressive to say the least, and it was possible just because we took great care in proving a useful theorem that would allow us to design a better algorithm. However, we can do even better.

To see that claim, observe that if algorithm 9.9, traverses the graph from v_0 in figure 9.1, then it will first traverse from v_0 to v_1, then from v_0 to v_2, doing the traversal from v_0 to v_1 again, then from v_0 to v_3, doing the traversal from v_0 to v_2 again, doing the traversal from v_0 to v_1 again, etc.

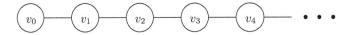

Figure 9.1: Traversing the graph for connectivity

In order to avoid these multiple traversals, we can use the fact that if there exists a path from v to u going through t, and a path from t to w, then there exists a path from v to w. Thus, instead of searching for a path from v in each iteration, we can search from any vertex that has a path from v. We show the resulting algorithm only for the vertex-centered abstract data type.

Algorithm 9.10.
Input: A graph G with at least one vertex, and with all vertices unmarked.
Output: A Boolean value indicating whether G is connected or not.
Side effect: Marks every vertex reachable from vertex number 0.
Algorithm:

1. *Use the operation* **VERTEX**$(G, 0)$ *to obtain the 0th vertex of G, and store the result in the variable named v.*

2. *Call the function* **mark_from** *(defined below), passing it G and v as arguments.*

3. *Use the operation* **VERTEX_COUNT**(G) *to obtain $|V(G)|$, and store the result in the variable named vc.*

4. *For i from 0 to vc − 1 do*

   (a) *Use the operation* **VERTEX**(G, i) *to obtain the ith vertex of G, and store the result in the variable named w.*

   (b) *Use the operation* **VERTEX_MARKED**(w) *to check whether the vertex w is marked.*

(c) If w is not marked, return with the value false.

5. If we come here, then every vertex is marked. Return with the value true.

Now, we must define the function `mark_from`. It is just another algorithm that takes a graph G and a vertex v as input, and which marks every vertex u of G such that there is a path between v and u.

Algorithm 9.11. *Input: A graph G with all vertices unmarked, and a vertex v.*
Output: None.
Side effects: Mark every vertex with a path from v.
Algorithm:

1. *Use the operation* `VERTEX_MARKED`(v) *to check whether the vertex v is marked.*

2. *If it is marked, then do nothing.*

3. *Otherwise:*

   (a) *Use the operation* `MARK_VERTEX`(v) *to mark the vertex v.*

   (b) *Use the operation* `EDGE_COUNT`(G, v) *to obtain the number of edges incident to v in G, and store the result in the variable named ec.*

   (c) *For i from 0 to $ec - 1$ do:*

      i. *Use the operation* `EDGE`(G, v, i) *to obtain the ith edge incident to v in G, and store the result in the variable named e.*

      ii. *Use the operation* `FOLLOW_EDGE`(G, v, e) *to obtain the other vertex incident to e in G, and store the result in the variable named w.*

      iii. *Call* `mark_from` *recursively with G and w as arguments.*

Let us examine the complexity of algorithm 9.10. Each vertex is visited at most twice; once to mark it, and a second time to check whether it is marked. Each edge is visited at most twice; once to discover that the other extreme is not marked, and a second time to discover that the other extreme *is* marked.

This analysis gives a complexity of $O(|V(G)|+|E(G)|)$; i.e., the execution time is proportional to the number of vertices and the number of edges of the graph. This result certainly represents an improvement of a factor 10^5 with respect to algorithm 9.9 on the example given above. Thus, if algorithm 9.9 is able to give an answer to our telecommunications company in roughly 17 minutes (10^3 seconds), then algorithm 9.10 is able to do the same thing in 10^{-2} seconds, or 10 milliseconds. Comparing this to our initial algorithm with an execution time of 30 years, we now have an improvement that is more than considerable; it is downright spectacular.

Perhaps the cited improvements might appear to the reader to be *too* spectacular to be realistic. However, it is quite common to observe such improvements between a bad and a good algorithm. In a case known to the author, a colleague was able to improve the main algorithm used by a company from around a week to a few seconds on typical problems used by this company.

In fact, it is often the case that programmers without any theoretical training develop software solutions with bad performance for problems, simply because they do not have the knowledge in theoretical computer science required to find an efficient solution. The result is often mediocre, with losses in the millions of Dollars or Euros. The possible savings to the company as a result of hiring relatively unqualified programmers have thus been lost many times over.

9.4   Eulerian graphs

In this section, we design an algorithm that determines whether a graph is Eulerian or not. (See definition 6.1.) We use only the vertex-centered abstract data type.

We know from theorem 6.2 in section 6.4 that in order for a graph to be Eulerian, it must be connected, and the number of vertices with an odd degree must be 0 or 2. In section 6.5, we learn that those conditions are also sufficient. From section 9.3, we know how to determine whether a graph is connected, and from section 9.1 we know how to compute the degree of a vertex. We can use the following algorithm to determine the number of vertices with odd degree:

Algorithm 9.12.
Input: A graph G.

Output: The number of vertices with an odd degree.
Algorithm:

1. *Initialize an accumulator to 0.*

2. *Use the operation* **VERTEX_COUNT***(G) to obtain* $|V(G)|$*, and store the result in the variable named vc.*

3. *For i from 0 to vc − 1 do:*

    (a) *Use the operation* **VERTEX***(G, i) to obtain the ith vertex of G, and store the result in the variable named v.*

    (b) *Call algorithm 9.2 to compute the degree of v in G, passing it G and v, and putting the result in the variable d.*

    (c) *If d is odd, then increment the accumulator.*

4. *Return the value of the accumulator.*

Using algorithms 9.12 and 9.10 it is now easy to design an algorithm for checking whether a graph is Eulerian. The details are left as an exercise.

9.5 Exercises

Definition 9.3. *A* loop *is an edge with a single incident vertex.*

Exercise 9.1. *Using the vertex-centered abstract data type, write an algorithm that counts the number of loops in a given graph G.*

Definition 9.4. *A* multiple edge *of a graph* $G = (V, E, \phi)$ *is an edge e such that* $\exists f \in E$ *such that* $e \neq f, \phi(e) = \phi(f)$*.*

Exercise 9.2. *For the vertex-centered abstract data type, write an algorithm that counts the number of multiple edges in a graph G.*

Exercise 9.3. *For the edge-centered abstract data type, write an algorithm that counts the number of multiple edges in a graph G.*

Definition 9.5. *We define a* Hamiltonian cycle *in a graph G to be a cycle $C = v_1, e_1, v_2, e_2, \ldots, v_n, e_n, v_1$ such that $\{v_1, v_2, \ldots, v_n\} = V(G)$ and $\forall i, j \in [1, n], v_i = v_j \Rightarrow i = j$.*

In other words, the cycle must contain every vertex of the graph, and each vertex must occur exactly once in the cycle. However, there is no obligation that each edge be included in the cycle.

Exercise 9.4. *Prove that a Hamiltonian cycle can not contain a loop. (See definition 9.3.)*

Exercise 9.5. *Write an algorithm that searches for a Hamiltonian cycle in an arbitrary graph G.*

Exercise 9.6. *Prove that in an undirected tree (See definition 7.9.), between any two vertices, there is at most one path.*

Exercise 9.7. *Simplify algorithm 9.8 for the case when it is known that the input graph is an undirected tree. (See definition 7.9.)*

Part III

Programming

Chapter 10

Programming

In order to appreciate the usefulness of the methods and techniques discussed in this part of the book, the reader should first get an idea of the reality of the software industry. We speak about the activity called "programming" in the software industry by which we mean the creation of software applications to be commercialized and sold either to other companies or to individuals.[1] The purpose of this chapter is to give the reader such an idea.

10.1   The software life cycle

In the literature, the *life cycle* of a software system is often spoken of. What is meant is all the phases that are part of developing the software system, from establishing the requirements that the client has for the system, to finalizing the system as a product, and ultimately to take the system out of service, perhaps in favor of an improved one.

The life cycle involves different activities in different phases of development, in particular:

- Analyzing client requirements.

---

[1]There is of course a lot of programming activity going on outside the software industry, in the form of so called FLOSS (Free, Libre, Open-Source Software).

- Designing the general architecture of the system.

- Designing individual modules of the system.

- Programming.

- Verifying each module (unit tests).

- Verifying the system (integration test).

- Correcting detected defects.

- Documenting the system.

- etc.

Those activities are not listed chronologically. Correcting defects is often mixed together with programming or design, and writing documentation is an activity that is often done in parallel with other activities. The reader can probably think of other overlapping activities.

In addition, the life of a software system does not end when it has been delivered to a client or sold to a customer in a store. It continues to evolve in different ways. Defects may be corrected after delivery and the corrections delivered to clients or made available for download. New functionality may be added. New versions may be created. The activities that occur after the first delivery of the first version of the software are collectively called *maintenance*.

According to many sources in the literature, maintenance activities are often responsible for some 80% of the total cost of the system. Of the activities occurring after delivery, adding new functionality is usually the one that takes the most time and effort. In order to facilitate the maintenance activities, it is imperative that the software be *well written* and *maintainable*. In addition, a company might use the same software module in different products, in which case those modules must also be *reusable*.

While the details of the requirements for software to be maintainable and reusable are outside the scope of this book, we will discuss a small part of the rules to be applied for writing maintainable software.

10.2 Purpose of the programming activity

After what was said in the preceding sections, we can now ask ourselves what the purpose might be of programming as an activity for software development. To the beginner, this question might seem very strange, because, after all, the purpose of programming is to write a program (sequence of instructions) that conforms to its specification, i.e., a program that does what it is supposed to do.

Nevertheless, the answer is not that simple. The programming activity has several objectives:

- The program should be correct; i.e, it should conform to its specification.

- It should be efficient; i.e., it should use efficient algorithms.

- It should be maintainable and reusable.

- It should be easy to use.

- The cost of writing it should be low.

- It should have as few defects as possible, or in other words, the quality should be high.

- The time to write it should be short.

Many of those objectives are contradictory. Methods for determining a reasonable compromise of these objectives are studied by a discipline related to computer science known as *software engineering*.

In this book, the main objective we will aspire to is that of maintainability. Why put maintainability ahead of conformity to specification? The reason is that:

- A program which is maintainable but incorrect can (thanks to its maintainability) be corrected relatively easily so that it conforms to its specification, whereas

- A program that is correct but not very maintainable must often be thrown away, with the effort of writing it wasted, when new functionality is added.

In this book, we discuss a small aspect of maintainability known as *readability* or *understandability*. This aspect of maintainability determines the ease with which a programmer can read and understand the program.

It is thus desirable to think of the programming activity as an *act of communication between two people*, namely the person writing the program, and the person attempting to understand it by reading it. During the development of a software system, the programmer must first of all keep in mind that it should be understandable by the person who will ultimately read the program. In this book, this desire to write an understandable program is the main objective of the programming activity that we discuss.

10.3   Shared culture

It might appear to be difficult to determine whether a program is understandable when we do not know the person who will read it, nor the knowledge of that person. Most often, in fact, when writing a program, the programmer does not know who that person might be, simply because the people that will maintain the software have not been chosen yet, and perhaps not even hired.

To complicate the maintenance of the software even more, the initial programmer will often change positions within the company, or even leave to go to a different one. This mobility is due to normal staff turnover in the software business. It is rare that a programmer stays at the same company for more than a few years.

Under these conditions, how can one determine universal rules in order for a program to be understandable?

The answer lies in a concept that we call *shared culture* among programmers. In fact, all developers should have the same basic training. This training is partially transmitted as part of courses given at the university level. But such courses are not sufficient for creating a shared culture among software developers.

In order to understand why, let us make a comparison between a software developer and an artist, say, a novel writer. The two are, in fact, very similar in many respects. The training of a writer includes the languages used to write the stories, methods for characterization, techniques of plot development, and other narrative skills. But a novel written by a person who has done nothing other than participating in this training would probably be fairly mediocre. The training of the writer is complemented by reading and understanding novels written by other authors, often as many as a hundred or more novels per year.

The situation is the same for a software developer. The initial training includes several programming languages, ways of organizing the instructions of a program so that it is efficient (algorithms and data structures), and rules of software engineering that are required for a maintainable and reusable program. But as with the novel writer, a program written by someone with only this training will probably be very mediocre indeed. The training of the programmer must be complemented by *regular reading of programs written by experts*, preferably several dozen such programs per year, and preferably using different programming languages.

This way, it is possible to create a shared culture, i.e., a way of expression that is common to all developers. A large part of this culture consists of something that we call *programming idioms*. In order to explain what a programming idiom is, it is again useful to make a comparison with natural languages. The grammar of a natural language such as English determines what phrases are considered *grammatical*. But it is not because a phrase is grammatical that it is actually used by speakers of that language. The phrases that are actually used represent a tiny subset of all the grammatical phrases, and these are what we call the *idiomatic phrases* of the language. For a simple example, in English, both "tooth brush" and "dental brush" are grammatical phrases, but only "tooth brush" is used. With "tooth floss" and "dental floss", it is the same, except that there, the opposite choice was made. Furthermore, one might one day visit the "eye doctor", but not the "tooth doctor". Instead, you visit the "dentist". It is important to realize that the choices of what grammatical phrases are idioms are somewhat arbitrary. There is no linguistic reason for having chosen one or the other. A question (which might be asked by a non-native speaker of English) such as "why can I say tooth brush, but not tooth floss", can only be answered by "because that is the way it is". There may be no logical explanation, only an explanation based on history and what choice by chance happened to win in the end. In order to establish some efficient communication with another person, it is important to restrict oneself to idiomatic phrases. Using non-idiomatic phrases will confuse the reader so that the reader will at best have to pause and think about what it is that the writer is trying to say, and in the worst case, the reader may misunderstand what was being said, a situation which in some cases can have serious consequences.

In programming, there is very much the same contrast between grammatical and idiomatic phrases. The grammatical phrases of a programming language are those that the *language standard* says are valid, and that therefore a (correct) compiler should accept. As with natural languages, the phrases that are actually used by programmers represent a tiny subset of the grammatical phrases, and for exactly the same reasons, and those are the *idiomatic phrases* of the programming language. Remember that writing a program is mainly to be seen as an *act of communication* between the author and the (future) maintainer. As with natural languages, it is important that this communication be as smooth as possible. To ensure that level of communication, the author must use only idiomatic phrases. Using other phrases will at best waste the time of the maintainer because of the additional effort it takes to decipher what was meant, and in the worst case result in the maintainer misunderstanding the intentions of the author, a situation which will invariably lead to program defects, possibly with serious consequences as a result.

Example: To express that a loop is to be executed n times using the programming language C, the programmer would always write it like this:

```
for (i = 0; i < n; i++)
   ...
```

A mistake often made by beginner programmers of C is to write like this:

```
for (i = 1; i <= n; i = i + 1)
   ...
```

The result (with certain restrictions) is the same, but the second phrase is not idiomatic. In fact, to the expert maintainer, this phrase gives an impression of the author having a "foreign accent" and that the "native language" of the author is probably Pascal or Fortran. This effect is identical to the reaction of a native speaker of English hearing a phrase such as "I have hunger" instead of "I am hungry", a choice which gives reason to suspect that the native language of the author might be French.

10.4 Basic programming rules

In order that the reader start to become accustomed to some basic rules of programming, in this chapter we discuss some such rules together with the reasons for their existence. Later, in chapter 12 we apply those rules to the particular case of the programming language Python used in this book.

As mentioned before, we will concentrate on a few rules for making a program understandable.

10.4.1 Uniform spacing

By *spacing* we mean the number of blank (space) characters to use:

- Before or after an operator such as '+' or '='.

- Before or after a comma in a list of items. Such items might be arguments to a function or variable declarations.

- Before or after an open or closing parenthesis, for instance, of an argument list.

- Before or after an open or closing bracket, for instance, of an array index.

- Before or after an open or closing brace.

In order for a program to be considered *readable* such spacing must at the very least be *uniform*, i.e., the same everywhere in the program. One may ask why this uniformity is important. Here are some answers:

- Some (many in fact) readers are distracted by the absence of spacing rules. This is enough of a reason to have such a rule, because distracting the reader means slowing down the communication, with loss of time, effort, and ultimately money as a result.

- The developer of a program in which uniform spacing is not applied gives an impression of being disorganized. This is the so-called *teenage-room effect*. It is difficult to imagine that a program of a disorganized person is, in fact, correct.

- Beginners often think that the only reader of the program is the *compiler* for the programming language. This assumption is incorrect in general. In a programming environment, such as UNIX or GNU/Linux, programmers frequently use tools such as `grep`, `awk`, `sed`, `Emacs`, etc., in order to process program code. These tools are often much more sensitive to spacing than the compiler. Non-uniform spacing can complicate the use of such tools, or in the worst case, may make them totally worthless.

Some developers think that spacing is a matter of personal taste, but in fact, it is one of the elements of the shared culture between developers. A developer who does not respect the spacing rules of the community, or who writes programs with non-uniform spacing, will be considered by the more experienced colleagues as a bad developer.

10.4.2   Uniform and economic indentation

By *indentation*, we mean the number of blank characters at the beginning of a line in a program. An experienced developer uses indentation to communicate the general structure of the program to the maintainer. It is, for instance, normal to increase the indentation of the statements in the body of a loop, so as to show clearly that every one of those statements is executed at each iteration of the loop.

Luckily, the language Python, chosen for this book, imposes severe rules of indentation. (See chapter 12.) The reader who already works (or is thinking of working) with other programming languages should, nevertheless, take note of these rules. Even if the language being used does not impose any restrictions on indentation, it is mandatory to establish such rules and to respect them faithfully.

Some readers of this book have perhaps been exposed to *professional* programs (i.e., programs having been written by programmers whose salaries come essentially from the activity of developing software) in which indentation and often also spacing are not uniform. This anomaly does not show that uniform indentation is optional, but instead that a large number of professional programmers are not *expert* programmers. In fact, in the field of software development, the adjective *professional* is not necessarily associated with *quality*. The reason for that disparity is very likely that so many professional software developers have no training in computer science.

By *economic indentation* we mean that the indentation must not waste too many blank characters at the beginning of the line. But why is this important? In fact, too many blank characters at the beginning of the line may require an instruction to be broken into two lines, and breaking instructions into several lines will increase the total number of lines. Since the number of lines that can be displayed simultaneously on a screen is fixed, there are then fewer instructions visible simultaneously, so that the maintainer can see fewer instructions. And when the maintainer can see fewer instructions, the program is automatically less readable, because it is important for readability that as large a portion of the program as possible be visible simultaneously (without compromising the other programming rules).

Most coding standards advocate using between 2 and 4 spaces for each level of indentation. A single space is not enough, and more than 4 are rarely needed. In some environments, a tabulation character is used for indentation, especially in environments where tab stops correspond to every fourth column. But this practice can create problems when the program is moved to a different environment.

10.4.3 Choice of identifiers

The *identifiers* of a program are the names used for variables, functions, types, classes, and other elements. These identifiers should be immediately understandable to the maintainer of the program. In mathematics (and in theoretical computer science as illustrated in the first part of this book), it is common to use identifiers with a single character, such as v, e, n, or i.

In programming, one must be more careful. In general, a good programmer prefers to choose more significant identifiers often with several words such as `additional_vertex`, `incident_edge`, `number_of_cases`, etc. In addition, no matter what the native language of the programmer might be, it is typical for identifiers to be in English. The reason is that it is more and more common for a development team to have an international composition, and English is the preferred language when it comes to software development. It is, in fact, common that companies based in countries where English is not the official language still have a company-wide rule that all communication must be in English, and this rule includes the act of programming.

In describing identifiers, we used the word *significant*, but in order to be significant, an identifier does not necessarily have to have many characters in it. The shared culture of developers has, in fact, developed some *habits* with respect the use of short identifiers.

Examples:

- The identifiers `i`, `j`, and `k` are used as loop counters.

- The identifier `m` and `n` are often used to indicate the number of iterations of a loop.

- Often when the *scope* is relatively small, it is common to use the first letter of the type as an identifier such as `v` for a vertex, `e` for an edge, `p` for a person, etc.

- Some identifiers are practically standardized in certain programming languages, such as `argc`, `argv`, and `fd` in the C language, or `self` in many object-oriented languages.

10.4.4   Comments

Every programming language has the possibility of inserting messages into the program text that are exclusively meant for the maintainer, and the compiler does not even analyze these messages. These messages are called *comments*.

It is common to think that the readability of a program increases with the number of lines of comments, but this belief is false in general.

First of all, it is important to realize that the contents of the comments can not be verified by the compiler. The consistency between comments and the program code is thus the responsibility of the programmer. And like every situation where a human is in charge, errors can be introduced. The programmer must thus verify that the comments are faithful to the code they comment. In the first version of a program, this consistency is relatively easy to obtain, because the comments are written based the code. During maintenance, however, the program code is modified, and then ensuring consistency becomes more difficult. Frequently, the code is updated by the maintainer without any attention paid to the comments, so the comments are not updated. The result is a situation (that is unfortunately very common) in which code and comments no longer correspond.

In order to avoid this problem, we advise the programmer to avoid *redundant comments*, i.e., comments that do not really help anyone understand the code. A special case of redundant comments is that of *paraphrasing*; that is, comments that repeat in English the direct low-level meaning of the code.

Examples:

```
i = 0 # set  i to zero
i = i + 1 # increment i
```

This type of comment should be avoided, because the comments paraphrase the exact meaning of the code.

Another type of redundant comments (unfortunately often practiced by professional developers) is the *function comment*. This type of comment precedes a function or a procedure, and explains the name of the function, the number and type of its parameters, etc. In general, this type of comment gives a clean and orderly impression. Unfortunately, it is also a source of confusion. It is not uncommon that the number, type, or order of the parameters to a function change over time, and when that happens, the function comment automatically becomes inconsistent with the program code. After each modification of the code, the programmer must therefore manually verify the consistency of the comment. When time and cost is a premium, this verification is often omitted.

So what is a good rule to follow in writing comments? Simple: A comment is desirable whenever it simplifies the understanding of the program by the maintainer. Before writing a comment, the programmer must then imagine being the potential maintainer and check that the task of understanding the code becomes easier with the comment.

In summary, then, comments are *complements* to the code, and they are meant to be read by the same person who will read the code itself in an attempt to understand it, and that person is the maintainer. In no case is the comment meant to be read by a person who does not understand the program code itself.

10.4.5 Abstraction and duplication

An important aspect of readability of a program is that of *abstraction*. We can define abstraction as *the act of naming a piece of the program in order to avoid duplicating it.*

But why do we want to avoid duplication of program code? There are several reasons:

- When some program code is duplicated, the maintainer has to read and understand it multiple times. Avoiding duplication makes life easier for the maintainer.

- When the maintainer is required to update the code, perhaps because a defect was found that must be corrected, if there are multiple occurrences of the defective code (often with minor variations), then the maintainer must find every such occurrence, a task which can be a difficult. Because of the variations, it is often impossible to use automated tools, so large parts of the program must be inspected manually in order to find such near-copies. When duplication is avoided, the maintainer can feel confident that a single correction will eliminate the defect.

- Duplication increases the total size of the code. Each screen can thus display less real content when there is duplication. Again, it is preferable to allow the maintainer to display as much of the code as possible simultaneously.

- Duplication complicates *reuse* of the code. It is much easier to reuse a piece of code that is written in the form of an abstraction, such as a function or a class.

There are several types of abstractions possible:

- Control abstraction in the form of functions and procedures.

- Type abstractions, often in the form of classes.

- Syntactic abstractions in the form of macros.

In this book, the most important type of abstraction is the control abstraction. Essentially, whenever the same sequence of instructions is needed more than once, it is preferable to create a named function. The most important aspect of this abstraction is to give it a significant *name*.

10.4.6   Scope of identifiers

By the *scope* of an identifier, we mean the part of the program that can refer to that identifier. For instance, an identifier used for a local variable inside a function has the body of that function as its scope.

In order to maximize the readability of the program, the scope of each identifier should be as small as possible. The smaller it is, the less the amount of program code the maintainer has to examine in order to determine where and how the identifier is used.

This rule automatically implies that one should avoid, as much as possible, *global identifiers*, i.e., identifiers that are accessible everywhere in a program. The rule also implies that an identifier local to a *block* inside a function is preferable to an identifier local to the entire function.

10.5   Exercises

Exercise 10.1. *If you have already written a small program, look at it again in view of the rules discussed in this chapter. Does your program use uniform spacing? Does it use uniform indentation? Are the choices of identifiers good? Does the program contain any duplicated code? Does it have any redundant comments?*

Chapter 11

Programming languages

The most important tool for programming is without any doubt the *programming language* used. The features of the language are important, because those features determine the structure of the program, and the structure in turn determines the readability and maintainability of the program.

However, there exist programming languages that are specific to certain domains, such as databases, graphic interfaces, etc., here we discuss only *general-purpose programming languages*.

Different general-purpose programming languages have different features, even though it is possible to identify certain *categories* of languages that are similar. The choice of a language for a software-development project is thus not something to take lightly. A developer must master several, or even several dozen, general-purpose programming languages, or at least have an idea of their general structure. Knowing several different languages allows the developer to make a good choice of language, given the requirements of the project at hand.

There is a tendency among neophytes, and sometimes also among more experienced programmers, to cling to one particular programming language, often the first one the programmer was exposed to, at the exclusion of every other language. Psychologists have an explanation for this phenomenon as a general reluctance of people to learn new things. In fact, during the learning period, the person runs the risk of being considered incompetent by peers, whereas using something that is familiar gives the impression of security and the possibility of being admired by the peers.

A developer must at all cost resist this tendency. The field evolves so quickly that it becomes absolutely necessary to learn new things. A developer that clings to a particular programming language at the exclusion of all other languages that are unknown to him or her could thus be looked down upon by more experienced colleagues. In fact, it is preferable not to talk about the number of languages that one knows, but about the number of languages that one learns *per year*.

11.1   Syntax and semantics

When a developer wants to know about a programming language, he or she does not necessarily have to learn that language in detail in order to get an idea of what it resembles. The developer can just determine a list of features (or absence of features) of the language compared to similar lists of other languages.

In order to understand that practice, we must first know the elements of programming languages that are essential to software development. For that, we need to distinguish between the *syntax* and the *semantics* of the language. The syntax of a language has to do with the superficial form of the programs written in it. Syntax determines whether braces or keywords such as `begin` and `end` are used to delimit blocks of program code. The semantics, on the other hand, determine what the program *means*.

For a computer scientist, the syntax of the language is almost without any importance. In fact, one quickly gets used to a new syntax. There are, of course, languages where the syntax is extreme, for instance, excessively verbose (COBOL) or excessively terse (APL). But for the vast majority of languages, the syntax is not a problem. A computer scientist that wants so know about the syntax of a language will be interested in a very brief description of it, containing comparisons with other languages, both with respect to similarities, and with respect to aspects of the syntax that are significantly different from other languages.

Semantics, on the other hand, is *very* important. Often, the semantics determine whether it is easy to write maintainable programs. In particular, the semantics determine what styles of programming the language can handle, such as *imperative, functional,* or *object-oriented* programming.

11.2   Features of a language

There are several features of a language that make it possible to describe it briefly.

One can characterize the *syntax.* This characterization is often done with respect to other languages. If the syntax does not resemble that of any other language, one can give a brief description of the most important points.

A programming language that makes frequent use of *assignment statements,* also known as *assignment operators,* is known as an *imperative* language, and an important aspect of the semantics of a language is the *meaning of the assignment operator.* In certain languages the *identity* of an object is preserved by the assignment. When this is the case, we talk about *uniform reference semantics,* because the assignment operation manipulates *references* (also known as *pointers*). and not the objects themselves. Other languages define the assignment operation so that it *copies* the object assigned, in which case we talk about *copy semantics.*

Some programming languages require the programmer to free allocated memory explicitly when it is no longer used. In this case, we say that the language uses *manual memory management.* If, on the other hand, the language is responsible for freeing memory that is no longer used, we say that the language has *automatic memory management.*

Another semantic difference between languages has to do with the *types* (integer, character string, etc.) of the objects manipulated by the program. Some languages require that the type of the object stored in each program variable be known to the compiler, that is, known before the program is executed. Such languages are called *statically typed.* If in addition the programmer must indicate these types, we talk about *explicit typing.* If the language is statically typed, but the compiler takes care of determining the type of the variables, then we say that the language uses *implicit typing.* A language in which *variables* are not associated with types (implicitly or explicitly), but only the *objects* that are values of those variables is said to be *dynamically typed*.

A term that is often used to describe what kind of abstractions a language supports, and what programming styles are easy to use with a particular language is that of a *programming paradigm*. The main programming paradigms recognized are: *imperative programming, prodecural programming, functional programming, object-oriented programming,* and *logic programming*.

A language in which the main abstraction concept is a *procedure* is called a *procedural language*. Most traditional *imperative* languages are procedural. Typical examples of procedural languages are C and Fortran. Notice that even though a language such as C in fact calls the procedures *functions*, these functions are typically not functions in the mathematical sense, so it is still justified to call these languages *procedural*.

A language in which the main abstraction concept is a *function*, (i.e., a procedure with no *side effects* so that it does not modify the environment in which it was called), is called a *functional language*. Programming in such a language is a question of composing small functions into larger ones. Some examples of functional languages are ML, Haskell, and Miranda.

An *object-oriented* programming language is a language where the main abstraction tool is that of an *object*. Examples of object-oriented languages are Java, C#, JavaScript, and Self.

11.3 Other important language characteristics

When a programming language is chosen for a programming project, some important characteristics of it must be taken into account, other than the *features*. (See section 11.2.)

11.3.1 Acquisition cost

It might be necessary to acquire a license to use some language implementation. For some commercial implementation, it is not uncommon that a per-computer, per-processor, or per-user license fee must be paid.

However, for a commercial programming project, the acquisition cost is usually negligible compared to other costs involved, such as programmer salaries. Furthermore, it is often possible to negotiate a lower price if several copies are acquired.

Today, there are many excellent implementations of many programming languages that are provided as so-called FLOSS (Free, Libre, Open-Source, Software), a term which implies (among other things) that the implementation can be installed at no cost on as many computers as required.

11.3.2 Runtime cost

More important than the acquisition cost, the supplier of a programming language implementation sometimes requires a fee to be paid for each copy of a program developed with their system that is provided to a customer, also known as a *runtime fee*. This fee can become an important part of the sales price of the software to be developed.

In particular, such a practice is often incompatible with the development of software that is meant to be made available to download for free.

As with acquisition cost, it is sometimes possible to negotiate a lower runtime cost with the supplier, depending on the number of copies of the final application that are sold.

11.3.3 Language standard

When choosing a programming language for a programming project, it is important to be convinced that the language and/or the implementation will continue to be available in the future. If not, large amounts of program code might have to be rewritten in a different language later.

The best situation is when a language has an *independent standard*, meaning that an organization independent of the suppliers of the implementations has published a document that defines every detail of the language. Some examples of such organizations are ISO, ANSI, ECMA, or IEEE. When a language has such a standard, it is often (but not always) the case that there exist *several implementations* from different suppliers, so that if one supplier ceases to exist, then a different implementation of the same language can be acquired from a different supplier.

Sometimes a language implementation is available as FLOSS[1]. While this situation guarantees that the language and the implementation will continue to be available in the future, it is possible that the language might change in arbitrary ways, so that parts of the program code will have to be rewritten if a new version of the implementation is installed.

Some languages exist as a single implementation controlled by the same company that supplies that implementation. This is a potentially risky situation, where a large investment might be lost either because the company ceases to exist, or because it discontinues the product.

11.4   Features of certain programming languages

11.4.1   C

The programming language C is a traditional imperative language in the *Algol* family. It uses static and explicit typing. Memory management is manual. The language has a rich set of operators. It allows for abstractions in the form of procedures and functions, and (with great pain) it allows syntactic abstractions in the form of macros. The language is designed for *system programming*, i.e, low-level programming in which the programmer has complete control over the objects in memory. The language is less practical for application programming, but it is nevertheless often used for this purpose. Thanks to operations with a relatively low abstraction level, the code generated by most C compilers is quite fast.

---

[1]FLOSS stands for Free, Libre, Open-Source Software.

11.4.2 C++

The language C++ is an *object-oriented* extension of the language C. (See section 11.4.1.) More specifically, C++ is a *classed-based* object-oriented language. In a class-based language, the concept of a *class* is used do describe a set of *objects* of the same *type*. (See section 8.2 for a discussion about data types.) Thanks to classes, it is possible to obtain *polymorphism* essential to the creation of maintainable programs. Polymorphism helps minimize the knowledge some part of a program needs to have about some other part of a program, so that modifications can be restricted to a smaller part of the program.

The fact that C++ uses manual memory management is a disadvantage for application programming. However, the language allows great control over many aspects of the program, such as the semantics of assignment and parameter passing. This complexity makes the language somewhat hard to master.

11.4.3 Fortran

The language Fortran is one of the oldest languages still in use. From its creation it has been adapted to new programming styles, such as the use of dynamic memory allocation and of pointers. The latest version dates from 2010. It is an imperative language, which, thanks to its limited expressiveness, allows the compiler to generate very efficient code, especially for programs that make heavy use of arithmetic computations, also known as "scientific programs".

11.4.4 Java

Java is a fairly recent language. It has benefited from accumulated experience of other languages, and from research in the domain of programming languages. The result is a language that is fairly well adapted to writing applications. It is statically and explicitly typed. The syntax resembles that of C++. The semantics are totally different, though. Java uses *uniform reference semantics*, whereas C++ uses *copy semantics*. Java uses *automatic memory management*. The language has platform-independent compiled code, so that compiled code can be transported over a network for ultimate execution on a different computer.

11.4.5   ML

The language ML is a functional language that uses static, but implicit typing. Memory management is automatic. Thanks to static typing, the compiler is able to generate very efficient code, without requiring the programmer to declare types of variables.

11.4.6   Lisp

Lisp is, together with Fortran, one of the oldest languages still in use. Like Fortran, it has been in constant evolution. The current language standard dates from 1994. It is a dynamically-typed language. The syntax is particular, because it reflects the internal representation of the program, which makes *syntactic transformations*, also known as *macros* possible and practical. Lisp is known as a *multi-paradigm* language, because it supports several programming styles, such as *imperative*, *functional*, and *object-oriented*. Lisp is an *interactive language*, which is typically used through an *interaction loop*. Efficient machine code is generated by most implementations through the use of *incremental compilation*.

11.4.7   Other languages

Many other programming languages exist, of course. Some of them are *special-purpose* in that they are meant for a particular type of application. Examples of such languages would be SQL for data bases or PostScript for drawing pages. Other languages are so-called *scripting languages* meant to be used to program *extensions* of applications written in more conventional languages. Examples of such languages are Python and Ruby. Some languages were designed for Web applications, such as JavaScript that runs in web browsers and PHP that is used for server-side web applications.

New languages are invented every year. Most of them never become popular. Other languages gradually get replaced by more recent ones, perhaps better adapted to the task at hand. Yet others evolve to accommodate new features and programming styles, sometimes keeping the old name, sometimes with a new name. A good software developer must follow this evolution closely, so that he or she can make optimal decisions about what language to use for a particular purpose.

11.5 Exercises

Exercise 11.1. *If you already know a programming language, for each one, answer the following questions:*

- *Does the language have more than one implementation?*

- *If it has only one implementation, what company, organization, or person supplies the implementation?*

- *Does the language have a standard defining it?*

- *If the language has a standard, what company or organization published the standard?*

- *Who has the authority to publish revised versions of the standard?*

- *Does the same company or organization both supply an implementation and publish the standard?*

Chapter 12

The programming language Python

This chapter contains an introduction to the programming language Python which has been chosen to illustrate the programming concepts in this book.

Python was chosen because of its relative simplicity. In only a few minutes, it is possible to see the result of the execution of a program. Python can be used either *interactively* or through a *text editor* allowing the user to write more complete programs. The interactive mode is then use for *debugging*, i.e., running the program in order to search for and eliminate defects.

12.1 Synthetic description of the language

In the spirit of section 11.4, we now give a synthetic description of the language Python.

Python is a dynamically-typed programming language with automatic memory management. It is interactive in that it can be used with an interaction loop. The language is multi-paradigm, because it allows for traditional imperative programming, but also for functional and object-oriented programming. The syntax of Python is peculiar because *indentation is significant* and indicates

133

program structure, such as nested blocks of code.

12.2   Starting and stopping Python

As mentioned before, Python is an *interactive* language. This means that the programmer is in constant dialog with the system. The *interaction loop* is responsible for reading, analyzing, and executing lines of text typed by the programmer.

In order to start the Python system on a computer system where it has been installed, it suffices to type **python** to the prompt of the command interpreter (i.e., the *shell*) of the operating system. Assuming the prompt of your shell is **$**, here is an example of how to start the Python system.

```
$ python
Python 2.7.2+ (default, Oct  4 2011, 20:03:08)
[GCC 4.6.1] on linux2
Type "help", "copyright", "credits" or "license" for more info...
>>>
```

The execution of your shell is now suspended, and you are interacting with the Python system, as can be seen from the fact that the prompt is now the one of the Python system **>>>** and no longer that of the shell **$**.

To stop the Python system, type **^d** (i.e., control+d). To do that, press the key marked **Ctrl** (or similar) while simultaneously pressing the key **d**. This gesture sends an *end-of-file* message to Python indicating that you have nothing more to submit to it. Python then stops its execution, and the shell prompt appears again. On some systems, you might be required to type **quit()** followed by the **RETURN** or **ENTER** key.

12.3   Using Python in interactive mode

12.3.1   Simple statements

Once you have started the Python system, you can submit lines of text to it. In the simplest case, a line of text represents a single Python *statement*. Such a statement must respect the *syntax* of the language Python. The result of the execution is determined by the *semantics* of the language. A particular kind of statement is an *expression*. An expression is a combination of *constants* (such as numbers), *variables*, and *operators* (such as + for addition) that together indicate how to compute a *value*. If you type an expression followed by an end of line (usually the key **RETURN** or **ENTER**), the expression is *evaluated*; i.e., its value is computed and displayed by the Python system. Example:

```
>>> 3 + 4 * 7
31
>>>
```

It is thus possible to use Python as an interactive calculator. Here, the character '*' stands for the multiplication operator.

But not all statements are expressions, as exemplified by the *assignment* statement. The character '=' is used for assignment. Here is an example:

```
>>> x = 4
>>> 5 + x
9
>>>
```

Here, the first line *assigns* the value 4 to the variable **x**. The second line asks that the expression 5 + **x** be evaluated. The value of that expression is thus computed and displayed.

This all seems very easy. In fact, aside from the character used to indicate multiplication, the notation is very similar to standard mathematical notation. Caution, however: the *semantics* are very different from that of standard mathematical notation.

In order to understand how Python works (and most of the so-called *imperative* programming languages), one must realize that to a variable corresponds a *place* in the memory of the computer. The assignment operator puts a value in this place, whereas the evaluation of an expression accesses this value. In mathematics the following example would be a contradiction; in Python, it is perfectly legal:

```
>>> x = 4
>>> x = 5
>>>
```

The first statement puts the value 4 in the place associated with the variable x, and the second statement immediately replaces that value by putting the value 5 in the place instead. The value 4 is thus lost. In the assignment statement, the place (here a variable) is indicated on the left-hand side of the character =, and the value to put there is determined by evaluating the expression on the right-hand side. As a consequence, one can not write (as one can in mathematics):

```
>>> 4 = x
SyntaxError: can't assign to literal
>>>
```

Here, Python indicates a syntax error.

Observe that the expression on the right-hand side of an assignment is completely evaluated before its value assigned to the place on the left-hand side. It is thus possible to write statements such as:

```
>>> x = x + 1
>>>
```

which has the effect of incrementing (i.e., adding 1 to) the variable x. This is a consequence of the fact that the content is first accessed when the expression on the right-hand side is evaluated. As part of that evaluation, 1 is added to current contents of the variable. The value obtained (one more than the initial value of the variable x) is then assigned to the variable x.

12.3.2 Compound statements

Expressions and assignments are examples of *simple statements*. There are also *compound statements* that are characterized by the fact that they contain other statements. An example of such a compound statement is the conditional statement `if`. It allows the execution of one out of two other statements according to the value of an expression. Here is an example:

```
>>> x = 4
>>> if x > 3:
...      y = 2
... else:
...      y = 5
...
>>> y
2
>>>
```

In that example, we notice several things.:

1. The first line is a normal assignment statement.

2. The second line starts an `if` statement. The line ends with the character ':'.

3. For the third line, the prompt has changed, indicating that the statement is not yet finished.

4. Since it is a compound statement, we must *indent* the statement on the third line. This indentation marks the *then* part of the `if` statement, i.e., the subordinate statement that will be executed if the condition is true.

5. The *then* part can contain several subordinate statements indented to the same column. Here, there is a single statement, namely the assignment statement `y = 2`.

6. The `if` statement allows for an *else* part that is introduced by the keyword `else` followed again by the character ':'.

7. Just like the *then* part, the *else* part can contain one or several statements, again indented relative to the `if` statement itself.

8. In order to indicate the end of the `if` statement, in interactive mode, one must type an empty line. When the program is typed separately into a file, then a new statement, indented like the `if` statement, signals the end of the *else* part of the `if` statement and of the entire `if` statement.

9. Here, since the expression in the `if` statement is *true*, the value of y will be 2.

Another example of a compound statement is the `while` *loop*. A loop is a statement that allows the repeated execution of a sequence of subordinate statements.

Loops are one of the characteristics of imperative programming. In fact, it is possible to obtain every functionality possible for a computer by using only assignment statements, conditional statements, `while` loops, and arithmetic expressions. This fact is one of the important results of an area of computer science known as *computability theory*.

Here is a an example of a `while` loop:

```
>>> fac = 1
>>> i = 1
>>> while i <= 6:
...     fac = fac * i
...     i = i + 1
...
>>> fac
720
>>>
```

Here, we have used the `while` loop to compute the factorial of 6. On the first two lines, we find some *initializations* (i.e, the assignment of an initial value), to the two variables `fac` and `i`. The variable `fac` will ultimately contain the value that we want to compute. The variable `i` is *incremented* after each iteration of the loop. Such a variable is called a *loop counter*. The statements in the *loop* *body*, i.e., `fac = fac * i` and `i = i + 1`, are repeated as long as the value of the variable `i` is less than or equal to 6.

12.3.3 Function definitions

As mentioned in section 10.4.5, an important part of programming consists of constructing *abstractions*. Here, these abstractions take the form of Python *functions*.

A Python function is different in many ways from a mathematical function. A Python function simply contains a sequence of statements that will be executed when the function is *called*. The function may *return a value* to the caller of the function. Here is an example:

```
>>> def fac(n):
...     f = 1
...     i = 1
...     while i <= n:
...         f = f * i
...         i = i + 1
...     return f
...
>>> fac(6)
720
>>> fac(7)
5040
>>>
```

Here, we defined a function named `fac` with a *parameter* which is called `n`. The parameter works like a normal variable, except that it is initialized by the caller of the function, i.e., the statement that invokes the function. The last line of the function definition means that the value of the variable `f` will be returned to the caller as the value of the call. After the function definition, we see two different calls to it, the first one with an *argument* 6, and the second with an argument of 7. The argument to the function is the value that will be used to initialize the parameter.

The variables f and i, and the parameter n are *local variables*; i.e., they exist only during the execution of the statements of the body of the function. A variable that exists not only during the execution of a function, but also before and after that execution, is called a *global variable*. There can be a global variable and a local variable with the same name. They are two different variables (so there are two different places to store values), but they happen to have the same name. This possibility is illustrated by the following code (assuming the definition of the function fac above):

```
>>> f = 321
>>> fac(5)
120
>>> f
321
>>>
```

Here, the global variable f is initialized to 321. When the function fac is called, the local variable f in the function fac is used to hold the value of the factorial of n (here 5). But once the function fac returns, the global variable f still has its old value 321. Local variables are essential in programming, because they allow a function to be *autonomous*, i.e., its execution does not influence, nor is it influenced by, assignments to global variables.

A function can have several parameters, separated by commas:

```
>>> def exp(a, b):
...     e = 1
...     i = 0
...     while i < b:
...         e = e * a
...         i = i + 1
...     return e
...
>>> exp(2, 6)
64
>>>
```

This function computes the value a^b for any value of a and any integer $b > 0$.

12.4 Using Python from a file

The interactive mode of Python is excellent for testing functions in order to determine whether they work as intended. But the interactive mode is reasonable to use for defining functions only if they are very small. Even with a function of only a few lines, it is easy to make typing mistakes which require retyping the entire function.

Because of that hazard, it is common to work with *files* containing function definitions and definitions of global variables. Such a file is called a *module*. To create such a module, use a *text editor* such as Emacs.

If one uses Emacs to create a file named `utils.py` containing the following text:

```
def fac(n):
    f = 1
    i = 1
    while i <= n:
        f = f * i
        i = i + 1
    return f
```

then this file is a Python module with the name `utils`. In order to take advantage of this definition inside an interactive session with Python, we must *import* the module. There are two ways of importing a module. The first method is illustrated by the following code:

```
>>> import utils
>>> utils.fac(4)
24
>>>
```

With this method, the module is loaded, and global identifiers (here `fac`) are made available, provided that they are prefixed by the name of the module as in `utils.fac(4)`.

If one wishes to avoid having to use a prefix for the identifiers in the module, one can use the second method, illustrated by this code:

```
>>> from utils import fac
>>> fac(4)
24
>>>
```

With this method, the function `fac` can be used without a prefix.

12.5   Python coding style

As mentioned in section 10.4, there are some basic rules of programming involving (among other things) indentation, spacing, and naming of identifiers, and those rules are often specific to a particular programming language.

Here, we give some of those basic rules that are specific to the Python language.

12.5.1   Indentation

Each subordinate block should be indented 4 positions compared to the parent block. Old Python code sometimes uses 8 positions, but newly written code should use 4 position.

12.5.2   Spacing

Each Python operator should be surrounded by exactly one space on each side, so that we write `x = 2 * a + b` (rather than `x = 2*a + b` or `x=2*a+b`).

In a list of comma-separated items (such as a list of parameters, a list of arguments, or the elements of a Python list, set, or dictionary), each element except the last is immediately followed by a comma, and the comma is immediately followed by one space. Thus, we write `(a, 2 * b, c)` for an argument list, and `["hello", 234, "there"]` for a Python list.

12.5.3 Naming of identifiers

Identifiers that name ordinary variables or functions are written in all-lowercase letters. If the identifier contains several words, then they are separated by underscore '`_`'. For example, we write `vertex_count` rather than `VERTEX_COUNT`, `vertexcount`, or `VertexCount`.[1]

Classes are named differently from ordinary identifiers. Class names use so-called *studly caps* or *camel-case* naming convention, starting with a capital letter. In this naming convention, no underscore character is used, and instead, each word in the identifier starts with a capital letter. For example, we write `VertexCenteredGraph` rather than `vertex_centered_graph`.[2]

12.6 Exercises

Exercise 12.1. *Write a function* `is_prime_number(n)` *that returns* 1 *(true) if the integer* `n` *is prime and* 0 *(false) otherwise.*

Exercise 12.2. *Write a function* `binomial(n, p)` *that computes and returns the binomial coefficient*

$$\left(\begin{array}{c} n \\ p \end{array} \right) = \frac{n!}{p!(n-p)!}$$

Hint: Do not make direct use of the definition of binomial coefficient and the function `fac`*; that approach will make a very complex computation. Instead, use a a loop that computes the simplified fraction.*

---

[1]This naming style is also the traditional style for the C and C++ languages, and it has been adopted by many languages other than Python.

[2]Variations of this naming convention are used for the Java and C# programming languages, and recently also for some code in C and C++.

Chapter 13

Graph programming

In this chapter, we use the language Python to program some of the algorithms that we developed in chapter 9. We alternately use the two abstract data types.

Notice that although we have mentioned the asymptotic complexity of our algorithms, there is no guarantee that the operations that we have considered to be elementary can be executed by the Python system in constant time. In fact, for some of them, the claim is almost certainly false. And even if an operation executes in constant time, it still might not be very fast. All this depends on how the Python system was designed (a detail which we will ignore in this book).

The Python code that we show in this chapter is *not* necessarily idiomatic, because the purpose is not to illustrate idiomatic code, but to illustrate how graph algorithms can be implemented. Thus, for instance, a statement such as:

```
if v == edge_end(G, e, 1):
    acc = acc + 1
```

Can in fact be written:

```
if v == edge_end(G, e, 1):
    acc += 1
```

And even:

```
acc += v == edge_end(G, e, 1)
```

However, we ignore this possibility here in order to keep the code easy to understand for the reader who does not necessarily know Python very well.

13.1   Degree of a vertex

We start this chapter by implementing algorithms 9.1 and 9.2 for computing the degree of a particular vertex of a graph, using the edge-centered and vertex-centered abstract data type respectively.

13.1.1   Edge-centered case

The following code is an implementation of algorithm 9.1.

```
def degree(G, v):
    acc = 0
    for i in range(edge_count(G)):
        e = edge(G, i)
        if v == edge_end(G, e, 1):
            acc = acc + 1
        if v == edge_end(G, e, 2):
            acc = acc + 1
    return acc
```

The code closely follows the steps of algorithm 9.1, so that it loops for each edge and accumulates the contribution of each edge to the vertex v in the accumulator acc. The main difference between the algorithm and the code is that the code does not need the local variables *vc* and *w*. As a general rule, it is hard for the programmer to invent significant names for variables, especially when the code is much bigger than this one. As a result, when the code is equally understandable without the use of a local variable, then no such variable is used.

The Python construct `for ... in range(...)` is a loop where the loop counter takes on the n values from 0 to $n-1$ where n is the value of the expression of the range, here `edge_count(G)`.

13.1.2 Vertex-centered case

The following code is an implementation of algorithm 9.2.

```python
def degree(G, v):
    acc = 0
    for i in range(edge_count(G, v)):
        acc = acc + 1
        if v == follow_edge(G, v, edge(G, v, i)):
            acc = acc + 1
    return acc
```

Again, this code closely follows the steps of the corresponding algorithm, and again, some local variables used in algorithm 9.2 have been eliminated to obtain a more terse program.

13.2 Average degree

13.2.1 Edge-centered case

In the case of the edge-centered abstract data type, algorithm 9.3 of section 9.2 is easy to program, and the result is a function with constant complexity, because it uses only basic Python functionality and operations defined by the abstract data type.[1]

If the graph is empty (i.e, it has no vertices), by convention, we define the average degree to be 0. Here is the code:

---

[1] Again, it is possible that the Python system can not guarantee constant complexity.

```
def average_degree(G):
    vc = vertex_count(G)
    if vc == 0:
        return 0
    return 2.0 * edge_count(G) / vc
```

While we could have eliminated the local variable vc here, and replaced it with `vertex_count(G)`, this is not such a good idea because even though the operation `vertex_count` is a primitive operation, it might still take significantly longer than just accessing a variable, and if we eliminate the local variable, this operation will almost certainly be called twice; once to see whether it is 0, and once in the division.

Also notice the use of the constant 2.0 rather than just 2. The reason for this is that the division that follows is between two integers, and when both operands of a division are integers, the result is always an integer, which is not what is wanted here. By multiplying the first operand by 2.0 first, it turns into a floating-point number which is what we want in this case.

13.2.2   Vertex-centered case

In the case of the vertex-centered abstract data type, we follow algorithm 9.4 of section 9.2 closely in the code:

```
def average_degree(G):
    vc = vertex_count(G)
    if vc == 0:
        return 0
    acc = 0
    for i in range(vc):
        acc = acc + degree(G, vertex(G, i))
    return float(acc) / vc
```

That code makes use of the **degree** function as a subroutine.

Also notice in this code the use of an explicit conversion of an integer acc to a floating point number so that again the division gives a floating point number as a result. An alternative would have been to multiply `acc` by the floating point number 1.0 first, but our solution is preferred.

13.3 Connectivity

13.3.1 Vertex-centered case

The code in this section is based on algorithm 9.10 of section 9.3. That algorithm uses another algorithm as a subroutine, namely algorithm 9.11, called `mark_from`, and which is responsible for marking all the vertices reachable by a path from some vertex v. For that reason, we start by showing the implementation of the `mark_from` function:

```
def mark_from(G, v):
    if vertex_marked(v):
        return
    else:
        mark_vertex(v)
        for i in range(edge_count(G, v)):
            mark_from(G, follow_edge(G, v, edge(G, v, i)))
```

After calling the subroutine `mark_from`, algorithm 9.10 executes a loop to check that all vertices are marked. This check might be a useful thing to do in other algorithms, so we write an independent function for it. The code below returns 1 (*true*) if all vertices of the graph are marked and 0 (*false*) otherwise:

```
def all_vertices_marked(G):
    for i in range(vertex_count(G)):
        if not vertex_marked(vertex(G, i)):
            return 0
    return 1
```

Before we show the final function, we need a function to unmark all the vertices of a graph. It is quite simple to write, and its complexity is $O(|V(G)|)$:

```
def unmark_all(G):
    for i in range(vertex_count(G)):
        unmark_vertex(vertex(G, i))
```

With these new functions, it is easy to translate algorithm 9.10 into a function named **connected(G)** that returns 1 (*true*) if the graph **G** is connected and 0 (*false*) otherwise:

```
def connected(G):
    unmark_all(G)
    mark_from(G, vertex(G, 0))
    return all_vertices_marked(G)
```

13.3.2   Edge-centered case

In chapter 9, we did not discuss how to determine whether the graph is connected when the edge-centered abstract data type is used. It is reasonable to ask oneself whether one can use the same function for the edge-centered abstract data type as for the vertex-centered abstract data type. The functions **unmark_all(G)** and **all_vertices_marked(G)** both work for the two abstract data types, because they use only operations that are common to both.

However, the function **mark_from(v)** used for the vertex-centered abstract data type can not be used for the edge-centered abstract data type because it uses the operations **edge_count(G, v)** and **edge(G, v, i)** that are specific to the vertex-centered abstract data type.

Unfortunately, an operation equivalent to **mark_from(G, v)** can not be written as easily for the edge-centered abstract data type as for the vertex-centered abstract data type, because in the edge-centered abstract data type, there is no direct access to the edges incident to a vertex. This access can only be obtained by traversing each edge for each vertex. The complexity we end up with will thus be $O(|V(G)| * |E(G)|)$, instead of $O(|V(G)| + |E(G)|)$ for the vertex-centered abstract data type.

Here is the code:

```
def mark_from(G, v):
    if vertex_marked(v):
        return
    mark_vertex(v)
    for i in range(edge_count(G)):
        e = edge(G, i)
        if edge_end(G, e, 1) == v:
            mark_from(G, edge_end(G, e, 2))
        if edge_end(G, e, 2) == v:
            mark_from(G, edge_end(G, e, 1))
```

With this definition, the function for testing the connectivity of a graph will be written the same way for the edge-centered abstract data type as for the vertex-centered abstract data type, except that it will have a complexity of $O(|V(G)| * |E(G)|)$:

```
def connected(G):
    unmark_all(G)
    mark_from(G, vertex(G, 0))
    return all_vertices_marked(G)
```

13.4   Eulerian graph

As we saw in section 6.5, if a graph is Eulerian, it must be connected, and the number of odd vertices must be 0 or 2. (See theorem 6.3.)

We already have a function for determining whether the graph is connected (See section 13.3.), and we also have a function for computing the degree of a vertex. (See section 13.1.) We start with checking that the graph is connected, and if not, we immediately return 0 (*false*). Then we loop for each vertex, and start counting the number of odd vertices. As soon as we have more than 2 such vertices, we again return 0 (*false*). Since the number of odd vertices of a graph is necessarily even, when the loop finishes, we can safely return 1 (*true*) because then the number of odd vertices must either be 0 or 2.

13.4.1   Vertex-centered case

In the case of the vertex-centered abstract data type, we obtain the following code:

```
def eulerian(G):
    if not connected(G):
        return 0
    acc = 0
    for i in range(vertex_count(G)):
        if degree(G, vertex(G, i)) % 2:
            acc = acc + 1
            if acc > 2:
                return 0
    return 1
```

Notice the use of the Python operator % in this function, which implements the *modulo* operation, i.e., it returns the rest of the division between its first and its second operand. Thus when the degree of the vertex is *even*, the rest of dividing the degree with 2 is 0, which also means *false*, so the body of the if is not executed. On the contrary, when the degree is *odd*, the rest of dividing by 2 is 1 which represents *true* and the body of the if is executed.

Establishing the complexity of this function is a bit tricky. The complexity of the function connected is $O(|V(G)| + |E(G)|)$, and it turns out, the for loop has the same complexity, because the function degree has a complexity that is proportional to the number of edges incident to the vertex it is testing, and since every vertex is tested once, this gives $O(|E(G)|)$, but since there can be isolated vertices, and those are also tested, then we need to add $O(|V(G)|)$ as well, for a total of $O(|V(G)| + |E(G)|)$, which for the entire function gives a complexity of $O(|V(G)| + |E(G)|)$.

13.4.2   Edge-centered case

The same function can be used in the case of the edge-centered abstract data type as in the case of the vertex-centered abstract data type, but the complexity is not the same, because the complexity of the function `degree` is not the same in the two cases.

The function `degree` in the case of the edge-centered abstract data type has a complexity of $O(|E(G)|)$, so we now have a nested loop where the number of iterations of the outer loop is $O(|V(G)|)$ and the number of iterations of the inner loop is $O(|E(G)|)$. The total complexity for such a nested loop is $O(|E(G)| * |V(G)|)$ and this complexity will dominate over that of the function `connected` for a total complexity of $O(|E(G)| * |V(G)|)$ for the function `eulerian` in the case of the edge-centered abstract data type.

13.5 Exercises

Exercise 13.1. *For the case of the vertex-centered abstract data type, write a function* `vertex_with_degree(G, d)` *which returns a vertex with degree* `d` *of a graph* `G` *if such a vertex exists, and* `-1` *otherwise.*

Exercise 13.2. *For the case of the edge-centered abstract data type, write a function* `vertex_with_degree(G, d)` *which returns a vertex with degree* `d` *of a graph* `G` *if such a vertex exists, and* `-1` *otherwise.*

Exercise 13.3. *For the case of the vertex-centered abstract data type, write a function* `vertex_with_max_degree(G)` *that returns a vertex with the highest degree of all vertices in a non-empty graph* `G`. *If there is more than one such vertex, any one of them can be returned.*

Exercise 13.4. *For the case of the edge-centered abstract data type, write a function* `vertex_with_max_degree(G)` *that returns a vertex with the highest degree of all vertices in a non-empty graph* `G`. *If there is more than one such vertex, any one of them can be returned.*

Exercise 13.5. *Using the function* `vertex_with_max_degree(G)` *from the previous exercise, write a function* `max_degree(G)` *that returns the highest degree of any vertex in a graph* `G`, *and* `0` *if* `G` *is empty.*

Exercise 13.6. *Program the algorithms of the exercises in chapter 9, using both the edge-centered abstract data type and the vertex-centered abstract data type.*

Part IV

Appendices

Appendix A

Programming of abstract data types

In order to be able to use the algorithms in chapter 13, it is necessary to have a Python implementation of the edge-centered and vertex-centered abstract data types. Here, we give an example of one possible such implementation for each abstract data type.

The two abstract data types use the same classes `Vertex` and `Edge` for vertices and edges. These definitions, together with the definitions of the common operations `mark_vertex(v)`, `unmark_vertex(v)`, `vertex_marked(v)` `mark_edge(v)`, `unmark_edge(v)`, `edge_marked(v)` are defined in the module named `graph`. In this module, we have also added two function that allow for vertices and edges to be *labeled* so as to be easily distinguishable.

---
graph.py

```
# The Edge and Vertex classes are valid for both abstract data types,
# because they do not contain any information other than the label.
# As a consequence, an instance of these classes can also be present
# in several different graphs, possibly using different abstract data
# types.

class Edge:
    def __init__(self, label = 'no label'):
        self.label = label
```

157

```python
            self.marked = 0
        def __repr__(self):
            return '<Edge labeled: ' + self.label + '>'

    def mark_edge(edge):
        edge.marked = 1

    def unmark_edge(edge):
        edge.marked = 0

    def edge_marked(edge):
        return edge.marked

    class Vertex:
        def __init__(self, label = 'no label'):
            self.label = label
            self.marked = 0
        def __repr__(self):
            return '<Vertex labeled: ' + self.label + '>'

    def mark_vertex(vertex):
        vertex.marked = 1

    def unmark_vertex(vertex):
        vertex.marked = 0

    def vertex_marked(vertex):
        return vertex.marked

    # Some helper functions.

    def label(object):
        return object.label

    def change_label(object, new_label):
        object.label = new_label
```

The two modules **egraph** and **vgraph** contain the implementation of classes and operations that are specific to the edge-centered and vertex-centered abstract data type respectively. Both these modules start by importing the classes and operations of the common module. Following that, each of the specific modules defines the class `Graph`. In each module, this class contains *methods* for adding a vertex and an edge, because the way this is done depends on how the class is represented, and that representation is specific to each abstract data type.

Following the definition of the `Graph` class, each module contains the definition of the operations specific to each abstract data type, and finally, each module contains a utility function for displaying a graph.

─────────────────────── **egraph.py** ───────────────────────

```
from graph import *

class Graph:
    def __init__(self, name = 'no name'):
        self.name = name
        self.vertices = []
        self.edges = []
        self.phi = {}

    def add_vertex(self, vertex):
        for v in self.vertices:
            assert v <> vertex, 'vertex is already in graph'
        self.vertices = self.vertices + [vertex]

    def add_edge(self, edge, vertex1, vertex2):
        assert not edge in self.phi, 'edge is already in graph'
        self.edges = self.edges + [edge]
        self.phi[edge] = [vertex1, vertex2]

# Operations of the abstract data type

def vertex_count(graph):
    return len(graph.vertices)

def vertex(graph, i):
    assert i >= 0 and i < vertex_count(graph), 'invalid vertex number'
    return graph.vertices[i]

def edge_count(graph):
    return len(graph.edges)

def edge(graph, i):
```

```
        assert i >= 0 and i < edge_count(graph), 'invalid edge number'
        return graph.edges[i]

def edge_end(graph, edge, i):
    assert edge in graph.phi, 'edge is not in graph'
    return graph.phi[edge][i - 1]

# Utilities specific to this abstract data type

def display_graph(G):
    print vertex_count(G), "Vertices :"
    for i in range(vertex_count(G)):
        print vertex(G, i).label
    print "\n", edge_count(G), "Edges :"
    for i in range(edge_count(G)):
        a = edge(G ,i)
        print edge_end(a, 0).label,
        print " --", a.label,"--",
        print edge_end(a, 1).label
```

————————————————— **vgraph.py** —————————————————

```
from graph import *

class Graph:
    def __init__(self, name = 'no name'):
        self.name = name
        self.vertices = []
        self.psi = {}

    def add_vertex(self, vertex):
        assert not vertex in self.psi, 'vertex is already in graph'
        self.vertices = self.vertices + [vertex]
        self.psi[vertex] = []

    def add_edge(self, edge, vertex1, vertex2):
        assert vertex1 in self.psi, 'vertex 1 is not in graph'
        assert vertex2 in self.psi, 'vertex 2 is not in graph'
        for v in self.vertices:
            for ev in self.psi[v]:
                assert edge <> ev[0], 'edge is already in graph'
```

```
        self.psi[vertex1] = self.psi[vertex1] + [[edge, vertex2]]
        if vertex1 <> vertex2:
            self.psi[vertex2] = self.psi[vertex2] + [[edge, vertex1]]

# Operations of the abstract data type

def vertex_count(graph):
    return len(graph.vertices)

def vertex(graph, i):
    assert i >= 0 and i < vertex_count(graph), 'invalid vertex'
    return graph.vertices[i]

def edge_count(graph, vertex):
    assert vertex in graph.psi, 'vertex is not in graph'
    return len(graph.psi[vertex])

def edge(graph, vertex, i):
    assert i >= 0 and i < edge_count(graph, vertex), 'invalid edge'
    return graph.psi[vertex][i][0]

def follow_edge(graph, vertex, edge):
    assert vertex in graph.psi, 'vertex is not in graph'
    for ev in graph.psi[vertex]:
        if ev[0] == edge:
            return ev[1]
    assert 0, 'edge is not incident to vertex'

# Utilities specific to this abstract data type

def display_graph(G):
    print vertex_count(G), "Vertices :"
    for i in range(vertex_count(G)):
        v = vertex(G, i)
        print "Vertices accessible from", v.label, ":"
        for j in range(edge_count(G, v)):
            e = edge(G, v, j)
            print " --", e.label, "--",
            print follow_edge(G, v, a).label
```

The module `utils` contains utility code that is useful for both abstract data types. In particular, it contains a function `make_graph` which takes two parameters: a *graph class*, and a *list of paths*. In practice, when creating a graph using `make_graph`, we always use `Graph` as the first argument, because this is the name of the class of the graph to be used, independently of whether the `egraph` module or the `vgraph` module has previously been imported.

The second parameter requires more explanation. It contains a Python *list* of elements, where each element represents a vertex of the graph to be built. Let us call this list the *top-level* list. Each element of the top-level list thus represents a vertex, and it is itself a Python list, nested inside the top-level list. Let us call this list the *second-level* list. The first element of the second-level list is a string which must be unique, and which is considered the *name* or the *label* of the vertex. The remaining elements of the second-level list each represents an *edge*. The edge is represented as yet another Python list with exactly two elements. Let us call this list the third-level list. The first element of the third-level list is the label of the opposite endpoint of the edge. The second element of the third-level list is the *name* or the *label* of the edge. Here is an example:

```
[["Jim", ["Anne", "close"]],
 ["Anne", ["Bill", "very close"]],
 ["Bill"],
 ["Sid", ["Fi", "never met before"], ["Pete", "close"]],
 ["Fi"],
 ["Pete"],
 ["Jo"],
 ["Matt"]]
```

This example is a textual representation of figure 2.1 of section 2.2, in which the edges have been labeled with some indication as to the closeness of the relation. As the example shows, each edge is represented only once, but it does not matter in which vertex it is mentioned.

Here is the code for the `utils` module:

```
                          ──── utils.py ────

from graph import *

def make_graph(graph_class, paths):
    # Build a dictionary that maps vertex labels to vertices
    vertex_labels = {}
    for p in paths:
        vertex_labels[p[0]] = Vertex(p[0])
    # Create an empty graph
    graph = graph_class()
    # Add the vertices to the graph
    for label in vertex_labels:
        graph.add_vertex(vertex_labels[label])
    # Create and add the edges to the graph
    for p in paths:
        v = vertex_labels[p[0]]
        for link in p[1:]:
            w = vertex_labels[link[0]]
            e = Edge(link[1])
            graph.add_edge(e, v, w)
    # Done.
    return graph
```

Appendix B

Programming graph algorithms

With the preparations from appendix A, we can now implement the algorithms using the two abstract data types. In order to choose which abstract data type is wanted, we need to include the correct definitions into our programs. To make this choice, we include in the beginning of a module either the statement `from vgraph import *` or the statement `from egraph import *`.

The modules `valgo` and `ealgo` assemble the algorithms described in chapter 9 and programmed in chapter 13.

```
——————————————————————— valgo.py ———————————————————————
# Algorithms for the vertex-centered abstact data type
from vgraph import *

def degree(G, v):
    acc = 0
    for i in range(edge_count(G, v)):
        acc = acc + 1
        if v == follow_edge(G, v, edge(G, v, i)):
            acc = acc + 1
    return acc

def average_degree(G):
    vc = vertex_count(G)
    if vc == 0:
        return 0
```

```python
    acc = 0
    for i in range(vc):
        acc = acc + degree(G, vertex(G, i))
    return float(acc) / vc

def unmark_all(G):
    for i in range(vertex_count(G)):
        unmark_vertex(vertex(G, i))

def all_vertices_marked(G):
    for i in range(vertex_count(G)):
        if not vertex_marked(vertex(G, i)):
            return 0
    return 1

def mark_from(G, v):
    if vertex_marked(v):
        return
    else:
        mark_vertex(v)
        for i in range(edge_count(G, v)):
            mark_from(G, follow_edge(G, v, edge(G, v, i)))

def connected(G):
    unmark_all(G)
    mark_from(G, vertex(G, 0))
    return all_vertices_marked(G)

def eulerian(G):
    if not connected(G):
        return 0
    acc = 0
    for i in range(vertex_count(G)):
        if degree(G, vertex(G, i)) % 2:
            acc = acc + 1
            if acc > 2:
                return 0
    return 1
```

```
# Algorithms for the edge-centered abstact data type
from egraph import *

def degree(G, v):
    acc = 0
    for i in range(edge_count(G)):
        e = edge(G, i)
        if v == edge_end(G, e, 1):
            acc = acc + 1
        if v == edge_end(G, e, 2):
            acc = acc + 1
    return acc

def average_degree(G):
    vc = vertex_count(G)
    if vc == 0:
        return 0
    return 2.0 * edge_count(G) / vc

def unmark_all(G):
    for i in range(vertex_count(G)):
        unmark_vertex(vertex(G, i))

def all_vertices_marked(G):
    for i in range(vertex_count(G)):
        if not vertex_marked(vertex(G, i)):
            return 0
    return 1

def mark_from(G, v):
    if vertex_marked(v):
        return
    mark_vertex(v)
    for i in range(edge_count(G)):
        e = edge(G, i)
        if edge_end(G, e, 1) == v:
            mark_from(G, edge_end(G, e, 2))
        if edge_end(G, e, 2) == v:
            mark_from(G, edge_end(G, e, 1))

def connected(G):
    unmark_all(G)
```

```
    mark_from(G, vertex(G, 0))
    return all_vertices_marked(G)

def eulerian(G):
    if not connected(G):
        return 0
    acc = 0
    for i in range(vertex_count(G)):
        if degree(G, vertex(G, i)) % 2:
            acc = acc + 1
            if acc > 2:
                return 0
    return 1
```

Bibliography

[AHU83] Alfred V. Aho, John E. Hopcroft, and Jeffrey Ullman. *Data Structures and Algorithms.* Addison-Wesley Longman Publishing Co., Inc., Boston, MA, USA, 1st edition, 1983.

[Bir98] Richard Bird. *Introduction to Functional Programming using Haskell.* Prentice Hall PTR, 2 edition, May 1998.

[BJG08] Jørgen Bang-Jensen and Gregory Z. Gutin. *Digraphs: Theory, Algorithms and Applications.* Springer Publishing Company, Incorporated, 2nd edition, 2008.

[Bon76] John Adrian Bondy. *Graph Theory With Applications.* Elsevier Science Ltd, 1976.

[Bud91] Timothy Budd. *An introduction to object-oriented programming.* Addison Wesley Longman Publishing Co., Inc., Redwood City, CA, USA, 1991.

[BW88] Richard Bird and Philip Wadler. *An introduction to functional programming.* Prentice Hall International (UK) Ltd., Hertfordshire, UK, UK, 1988.

[CSRL01] Thomas H. Cormen, Clifford Stein, Ronald L. Rivest, and Charles E. Leiserson. *Introduction to Algorithms.* McGraw-Hill Higher Education, 2nd edition, 2001.

[Dow09] Allen B. Downey. *Python for Software Design: How to Think Like a Computer Scientist.* Cambridge University Press, New York, NY, USA, 1 edition, 2009.

[FFFK01]   Matthias Felleisen, Robert B. Findler, Matthew Flatt, and Shriram Krishnamurthi. *How to design programs: an introduction to programming and computing.* MIT Press, Cambridge, MA, USA, 2001.

[GY03]   J.L. Gross and J. Yellen. *Handbook of Graph Theory.* Discrete Mathematics and Its Applications. Taylor & Francis, 2003.

[JHM11]   Richard Jones, Antony Hosking, and Eliot Moss. *The Garbage Collection Handbook: The Art of Automatic Memory Management.* Chapman & Hall/CRC, 1st edition, 2011.

[Lut10]   Mark Lutz. *Programming Python, 4th edition.* O'Reilly Media, Inc., 2010.

[MRA05]   Alex Martelli, Anna Ravenscroft, and David Ascher. *Python Cookbook.* O'Reilly Media, Inc., 2005.

[MS08]   Kurt Mehlhorn and Peter Sanders. *Algorithms and Data Structures: The Basic Toolbox.* Springer Publishing Company, Incorporated, 1 edition, 2008.

Index

www.ingramcontent.com/pod-product-compliance
Lightning Source LLC
Chambersburg PA
CBHW080414060326
40689CB00019B/4239